GYMNASTICS
FOR
WOMEN

BROWN

PHYSICAL EDUCATION ACTIVITIES SERIES

Consulting Editor:

AILEENE LOCKHART
University of Southern California
Los Angeles, California

Evaluation Materials Editor:

JANE A. MOTT
Smith College
Northampton, Massachusetts

ARCHERY, Wayne C. McKinney
BADMINTON, Margaret Varner
BADMINTON, ADVANCED, Wynn Rogers
BIOPHYSICAL VALUES OF MUSCULAR ACTIVITY, E. C. Davis,
    Gene A. Logan, and Wayne C. McKinney
BOWLING, Joan Martin
CANOEING AND SAILING, Linda Vaughn and Richard Stratton
CIRCUIT TRAINING, Robert P. Sorani
CONDITIONING AND BASIC MOVEMENT CONCEPTS, Jane A. Mott
CONTEMPORARY SQUARE DANCE, Patricia A. Phillips
FENCING, Muriel Bower and Torao Mori
FIELD HOCKEY, Anne Delano
FIGURE SKATING, Marion Proctor
FOLK DANCE, Lois Ellfeldt
GOLF, Virginia L. Nance and E. C. Davis
HANDBALL, Michael Yessis
JUDO, Daeshik Kim
LACROSSE FOR GIRLS AND WOMEN, Anne Delano
BASKETBALL FOR MEN, Glenn Wilkes
GYMNASTICS FOR MEN, A. Bruce Frederick
MODERN DANCE, Esther E. Pease
PHYSICAL AND PHYSIOLOGICAL CONDITIONING FOR MEN, Benjamin Ricci
SKIING, Clayne Jensen and Karl Tucker
SKIN AND SCUBA DIVING, Albert A. Tillman
SOCCER, Richard L. Nelson
SOCIAL DANCE, William F. Pillich
SOFTBALL, Marian E. Kneer and Charles L. McCord
SQUASH RACQUETS, Margaret Varner and Norman Bramall
SWIMMING, Betty J. Vickers and William J. Vincent
TABLE TENNIS, Margaret Varner and J. R. Harrison
TAP DANCE, Barbara Nash
TENNIS, Joan Johnson and Paul Xanthos
TENNIS, ADVANCED, Chet Murphy
TRACK AND FIELD, Kenneth E. Foreman and Virginia L. Husted
TRAMPOLINING, Jeff T. Hennessy
VOLLEYBALL, Glen H. Egstrom and Frances Schaafsma
WEIGHT TRAINING, Philip J. Rasch
BASKETBALL FOR WOMEN, Frances Schaafsma
GYMNASTICS FOR WOMEN, A. Bruce Frederick
WRESTLING, Arnold Umbach and Warren R. Johnson

PHYSICAL EDUCATION
ACTIVITIES SERIES

GYMNASTICS
FOR
WOMEN

A. BRUCE FREDERICK

Wisconsin State University
Superior, Wisconsin

WM. C. BROWN COMPANY PUBLISHERS
DUBUQUE, IOWA

Printed in the United States of America

Preface

Within the past decade, we in the United States and other English-speaking countries have witnessed an unusual development in girls' sports. Gymnastics, an entirely feminine variety, has grown in prominence and is practiced and encouraged almost everywhere.

Two National Institutes on Girls' Sports have been devoted partially to gymnastics. High school teams and clubs are not rare. A dozen or more books have been published on gymnastic subjects and within a year or two another dozen are sure to appear. A special quarterly magazine, devoted to gymnastics for girls and women, has recently been initiated in California.* Clinics flourish. In summer gymnastic camps, girls may outnumber the boys as participants in a ratio as great as three to one!

Who would have predicted these things ten short years ago? At that time a modern gymnastic program for girls was virtually unknown, yet the rapid development of this activity is not surprising. Gymnastics for girls is one of those rare activities which qualifies as something more than a borrowed adaptation from the wide world of boys' sport. In gymnastics you can truly be a girl's girl.

With the help of this book, you will take your first gymnastic steps. The contents are designed to make you think as well as act. You might even dream a bit as you identify with a great Olympic champion, Vera Caslavska, whose grace and elegance have been captured and recorded for you on pages 57-60. You will be exposed to the interesting language of gymnastics and the philosophy and code of the International Gymnastic Federation.

---

*Mademoiselle Gymnast, Sundby Publications, P.O. Box 777, Santa Monica, Cal.

In Chapter 3, you will find the author's concept of your basic program for gymnastic skill development. Upon mastering the movements presented you will find immediate need for more complicated work. How nice to know that you may get that extra help today when only a decade ago it would have been almost impossible to obtain.

Self-evaluation questions are distributed throughout the text. These will afford you typical examples of the kinds of understandings and levels of skill that you should be acquiring as you progress toward the mastery of gymnastics. It would be well for you not only to answer the printed questions but to pose additional ones as a self-check on learning.

Since the order in which the content of the text is read and the teaching progression of the instructor are matters of individual decision, the evaluative materials are not necessarily positioned according to the presentation of given topics. In addition in some instances you may find that you cannot respond fully and accurately to a question until you have read more extensively or have gained more experience. From time to time you should return to such troublesome questions until you are sure of the answers or have developed the skills that are called for, as the case may be.

The author is especially indebted to one of his students, Rick Robson, for his willingness not only to help with the preparation of these pages but because he has been a particularly inspiring and idealistic young man who represents for the boys and girls of his acquaintance the best gymnastics has to offer.

A. Bruce Frederick

Contents

TO MY GIRLS . . .
L. B. AND A SWEET LITTLE THING
WE NAMED PAULA

What Gymnastics Is Like

Your body is a marvelous machine. As its manager-engineer you may regulate it almost as you wish. From the time you were beginning to walk your machine-like body has encountered many challenges. Running, jumping, walking, creeping, climbing, pushing and pulling are just a few of the thousands of movements you have attempted and mastered. You can probably think of some movements that you are currently trying to learn. Included, no doubt, are some gymnastic movements.

Gymnastics is the spice that adds a touch of interesting variety to movement. Each time you learn to do a new gymnastic movement, it's like learning to walk all over again. How wonderful to know that the joy you once experienced with your first step can be recaptured as you learn gymnastics!

Since you have been developing your mind as well as your body, the pleasures of movement may now be remembered. Do you remember your first step? If not, your parents can tell you about the pleasure you experienced at that moment. By now you take walking for granted unless that walk is mixed with gymnastic spice. A pirouette or a roll will do very nicely. You will enjoy gymnastics primarily because you will discover and experience new movements. Many of these movements are silly, impractical or could even be dangerous (if not properly executed) but you will love to do them. There need be no other purpose!

But gymnastics, unlike most of the world of sport, is unique because of the variety of ways it is enjoyed and applied. All ages and both sexes enjoy gymnastics. For girls and women the competitive and recreative aspects differ in objectives and scope from the corresponding program for boys and men. In Europe it is common to find housewife gymnastics or family gymnastics. In the United States we sometimes find synchronized gymnastics and ball gymnastics being performed by members of high school and college clubs.

The selection of the four international competitive events (floor exercise, side horse vaulting, balance beam and uneven parallel bars) was the result of a thorough reexamination of the special needs of girls and women. Exercises and apparatus demanding typically masculine strength were eliminated from the international program. Competitive gymnastics for girls and women therefore demands attributes of femininity. This is not simply a duplication of a typically masculine sport. In fact, most boys look pretty silly when they try to perform movements incorporated in girls' competitive routines just as many girls look silly when they attempt to perform activities which are typically for men.

Each of the four international events was selected for its singular contribution to feminine physical development. The gymnastic Olympians must do exercises in each event. From the start of your gymnastic participation, try to do a little work in each event even if competition is not your immediate goal. In this way you will enjoy the widest possible variety of gymnastic movements and obtain the maximum benefits of physical development through gymnastics. In short, be an all-around gymnast.

The total fitness values of gymnastics are great but bear in mind that human beings, unfortunately perhaps, are not highly motivated to do things which benefit their health. If they were, none of us would smoke; we would choose our foods a bit more carefully; we would always put on our seat belts and we would learn to relax and thus avoid many of the tension-induced disorders of modern living.

Fitness is the bonus of gymnastics. The girl who learns to do a handstand at age ten will, at regular intervals throughout her life, make the effort to see if she still can. She is proud of her accomplishment. In order to hold a handstand for any length of time you will have acquired a fine sense of balance. You will have the necessary muscle tone and muscle strength in your arms, shoulders and abdomen. Even your legs get a workout in a handstand although they do not support weight. These are fitness bonuses. You don't usually think about them. You will do your handstand for the sheer enjoyment of accomplishment not because it makes your "tummy" flat. You might join a fitness class or engage in a program of therapeutics which may result in the same physical development but you may soon be bored with a very elementary, though taxing, calisthenic routine. The recent addition of fitness parlors and commercial slim gyms in many communities with all of their chrome plated equipment, perfumed air and plush rugs cannot provide the interesting variety and joy that will be yours in gymnastics.

The bonus of muscular strength is often confusing to girls. Some believe that they will become highly muscular as a result of strenuous gymnastic participation; however, basic developmental patterns depend on the type of body inherited from parents. Since an overwhelming majority of girls develop traditionally feminine physiques, a strength-taxing regimen will ordinarily result in a more feminine girl not a "muscle-bound" mixture. In gymnastics, strength will be your silent partner; you will develop, use, and benefit from it. Girls who lack normal amounts of strength develop many problems because of their weakened muscular condition. Insufficient strength may actually detract from your feminine beauty and make movement of all kinds difficult and awkward.

A Hungarian doctor, a woman by the way, found that childbirth is exceptionally easy for women who are active in gymnastics and other sports. Especially noted was the relative ease with which these women handled their labor pains and the actual delivery phase. The great Russian gymnast, Larisa Latynina, has two children. She won the silver all-around gymnastic medal in the Tokyo Olympiad. Other studies point to the possibility that pains associated with the menstrual cycle are best handled by an active girl or woman.

To participate in gymnastics, all you need is space. Most beginners will first try simple tumbling and basic movement. As you develop your gymnastic competency you will need to find such things as mats and pieces of apparatus such as a beam or a bar. You will find some ideas in this book which will help you to simulate apparatus requirements but once you "catch on" gymnastically you will want and need the real thing!

As a modern girl, you are very fortunate to be living in an era of gymnastic expansion for girls and women. Many, many high schools, colleges and gymnastic clubs have recently obtained the kind of gymnastic equipment you will need. Perhaps you have noticed this renewed interest at your own school. You may have picked up this book for this reason.

If a gymnastic program of some kind has not already been started in your school or community, rest assured that it is only a matter of time before one might be. You can play a major role in getting a program started. It depends first of all on your interest and that of your friends.

Recent graduates in physical education will be prime sources of help to you since their undergraduate study has also been affected by the "new look" at gymnastics. Established teachers have been attending clinics and institutes in order to be ready for you when you are ready for the kinds of help you cannot get in this introductory book. It is the purpose of this book to help prepare you for the sport with spice, the spice of movement . . . gymnastics.

2

Preparation
For Gymnastics

You must prepare yourself in three primary areas in gymnastics. They are (1) the uniform and other personal equipment (2) knowledge and (3) physical qualities of strength, flexibility and power.

UNIFORM AND PERSONAL EQUIPMENT

From the very start of your adventure in gymnastics, you must understand the need for proper dress.

The leotard, named for a French circus acrobat, a man by the way, is most appropriate since it is light and permits free movement. When it is fitted properly, the leotard is not likely to become entangled while you work on apparatus. Its close fitting design has no part which will get into your line of sight or in any other way prevent you from performing the wide variety of movement combinations familiar to the gymnast.

Light slippers are preferred to conventional gymnasium or tennis shoes. The latter add excessive weight to the lower extremities and may prevent you from attaining the natural feeling required for most gymnastic movements. Some girls prefer to work barefooted. On the beam, you may wear a cotton "footlet."

You will need to get used to wearing hand guards. These protective devices, the gymnast's "gloves," are worn to prevent excessive friction. They are especially valuable as a preventative device for work on the uneven parallel bars. You should never work to the blister stage in gymnastics. When your hands feel very warm or begin to sting a bit, practice some other skills which do not involving gripping with the hands.

Which of these hair styles do you think suitable for the gymnast?

Evaluation Questions

HAIR STYLES FOR GYMNASTS

If you get used to wearing hand guards as a novice, they will not tend to be a distraction when you are learning the kinds of movements for which they are especially recommended.

Gymnastic chalk (magnesium carbonate) is available in most drug stores in small blocks. It is applied lightly to the hands as a friction preventative and it will absorb excessive perspiration.

Girls are especially conscious of anything which will result in unattractive hands. If you take the precautions suggested, your hands need not ever lose their natural, feminine attributes.

Chalk is occasionally applied to the hocks (backs of knees) when hanging from the "knees" in an exercise requirement. You may also wear tights or stretch pants when you practice skills in which knee hanging and other kinds of leg work is emphasized.

Your hair should be pulled back into a style which will prevent it from getting into your eyes. It should not obstruct movement in any way. Fingernails of the Fu Manchu variety are especially undesirable in gymnastics, as they are in most other sports. The writer has always encouraged girls to preserve and work for a natural, healthy appearance in gymnastics.

Subdued make-up is preferable to the gaudy variety. Natural or clear nail polish makes for a better gymnastic appearance. A bright-colored leotard is nice to see. Unless the material is quite heavy, light colored leotards, including white and pink, are undesirable.

KNOWLEDGE

To be a gymnast, you must prepare your mind as well as your body. Understanding and knowledge of what you are doing is essential. The

Diagram A:

HAIR STYLES FOR
GYMNASTS

fundamentals of such knowledge, with a special emphasis on mechanics, are presented below in outline form.

1. *Your Center of Gravity (C.G.).* Your C.G. is that elusive spot in your body which can truly be called the center of your weight. Since you can change your shape rapidly in gymnastics, you may not always know exactly where the C.G. is located. We may think of it, however, as being generally located inside the body at the level of the top of the hips. See Figure 2-1. The C.G. is an important consideration in the following kinds of gymnastic movement:

   a. Circles around a bar—It is important to remember that the C.G. should be stretched as far away from the bar as possible on the way down. In this way you will build up the greatest possible momentum since the force of gravity is working with you. On the way up, however, gravity works against you and you conserve your momentum by pulling your C.G. in towards the bar. In so doing you will speed up the movement and assure yourself of a completed circle. Bar circles therefore are not true circles since they must all have a shorter radius on the way up. See Figure 2-2(a). This represents the "circular" pattern of the gymnast in Figure 2-2.

   b. Circles whose paths are parallel with the ground—In this kind of circle, twist or spin, the force of gravity pulls evenly. In such circles, the axis of rotation passes through the C.G. To go slowly, you stretch away from this axis; to go quickly, you pull in towards the axis. Sit on the floor and try to spin around with your legs stretched out; suddenly tuck them in. What happened?

7

c. In balancing, the C.G. must be over the supporting base. The smaller the base, the more difficult the balance.

d. When spotting a gymnast, the weight is usually best controlled with a force applied near the C.G. or in the general area surrounding the hips. Spotting will be discussed in Chapter 4.

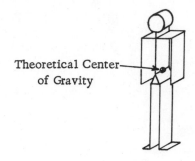

Theoretical Center of Gravity

Figure 2-1

Figure 2-2

Figure 2-2a.—Path of C.G. in knee circle

2. *What You Should Know About Newton's Three Laws.* Newton did so much more for us than to simply wait for that immortal apple to hit him on the head. As concerns forces, he taught us to be aware of three things:

a. Law I—While performing (or spotting) a movement, we must use a force to get action started. To stop the action we must again use a force. Ordinarily, we use either muscular force or the force of gravity.

b. Law II—(This law has greater applications in spotting. See Chapter 4.) Once a gymnast is in motion, you should look for opportunities to spot her in the direction of that motion. You can make her go faster (accelerate the movement) if you add some of your own muscle power at a time before she begins to slow down.

c. Law III—You must "cock" a gymnastic movement in the same sense as a gun is cocked. The cocking action is always opposite the direction required in the movement. This action produces a reaction in the opposite direction. Thus, we go down to go up; we go forward to go backward and we cast in one direction to do a circle in an opposite direction. Try jumping sometime without first "cocking" the legs. In the Caslavska Index in Chapter 6 you can read about and observe many examples of this law of action-reaction.

3. *Levers and Moments.* A lever is simply a bar (bone) which turns about a fixed point or fulcrum (joint) and is set into motion by a force (muscular). In all lever action there is a resistance to movement (body weight). The tendency for a body or bar to rotate about a fixed point when it falls out of balance is known as a moment. A moment is created by our bodies every time they fall out of balance. See Figure 2-3.

There are three kinds of levers:

a. A lever which favors force or strength.

b. A lever which favors speed and range. Most of the levers of your body are of this type. The muscles are attached to bones in such a way that the force arm is much smaller than the resistance arm. Remember, the longer you can make yourself and the more speed you can generate, the better you will perform. Is it any wonder that the coach will often say, "Point your toes!"? In doing so, the gymnast makes herself longer and takes advantage of her special leverage system. You don't simply point your toes for better form. See Figure 2-4.

c. A lever which may favor force, resistance or neither. This is the typical seesaw lever. You become a human seesaw every time you hold your body in a balance.

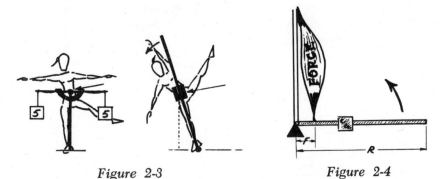

Figure 2-3   Figure 2-4

Figure 2-4.—Typical body lever

4. *Axes.* Your body has three major axes. Each passes through the C.G. Whenever you turn in the air, your body will rotate around one or more of these axes. (See Figure 6-2 in Chapter 6)

    a. The long axis—This is the axis which runs from head to feet through the C.G.

    b. The transverse axis—This axis runs from one side of the body to of these axes. (See Figure 5-2 in Chapter 5)

    c. The medial axis—This axis runs from the front of the body to the back of the body through the C.G.

PREPARATION OF THE BODY

The preparation of the body in flexibility and strength are most important for the developing gymnast. Teachers of ballet speak of "preparing the instrument." This thought is important to remember in your gymnastic development also. The outline of exercises which follows will help you to prepare and evaluate your progress in the development of flexibility and strength.

1. Flexibility

Flexibility represents the stretch component of the gymnast. Stretching is one of the two major functions of muscle tissue. The other is contraction. We will consider the latter under comments on strength.

To develop flexibility, you must apply pressure which will result in desirable stretching qualities. When pressure is applied, it should be applied with care; it should be applied sparingly as well as steadily, slowly and evenly.

The English coach and author, George Kunzle,[1] emphasizes steady pressure in the development of flexibility as opposed to "bouncy" or uneven pressure. In his book on floor exercise, he especially recommends the following kinds of gymnastic stretching:

—Toe pointing   —Hamstring stretching
—Splits   —Shoulder stretching
—Backbending

A. *Toe Pointing.* Notice B-15 and B-58 in the Caslavska sequences. The top of one foot is on the beam. Attempt the same foot position but place the supporting foot to the rear of the bent one. Now press the shin

---

[1]Kunzle, G. W. and B. W. Thomas, *Olympic Gymnastics—Vol. I—Freestanding.* London: James Barry (Pub.), 1956.

of the back leg carefully into the calf of the leg in front to add steady pressure to the toe point. Change the position of the feet and repeat. A "push-up" position (front support or front leaning rest) with the weight supported on the hands and tops of the feet will also be of value in developing toe point.

B. *Splits.* These typical gymnastic positions should be given careful consideration. If you are a natural "splitter" you will probably need to concentrate some of your conditioning time on strength exercises which work in opposition to the pull or stretch of the splits. It is very possible that you may be too loose! If you can't get all the way down on both sides, you will need to practice the splits every day. Notice B-19, B-34, B-70 and B-69 in the Caslavska sequences on the beam. She is shown passing through splits in these drawings. The splits are therefore important to develop for movements of many kinds as well as for use as static holds. You will find more about splits in the next chapter.

C. *Backbending.* A stiff-backed gymnast is seriously limited because a variety of movements require backbending flexibility. On the beam, unevens and the floor, you will find many examples of a backbending Caslavska. Notice that her back maintains a smooth curve rather than being extremely bent at the joints. Extreme flexibility is more a characteristic of the acrobat or contortionist than it is of the gymnast. See Figure 2-5. (Note: The white figure represents a reasonable extreme of backbending for the gymnast. The acrobat goes beyond this very often and is undesirable in gymnastics.

D. *Hamstring Stretching.* One example of this kind of stretch is shown by Caslavska in B-48 of the sequence drawings. Although she is holding a balance in this frame, she can be found in a similar stretch position at least eight times in the uneven bar sequence. In gymnastics, this "jackknife" position of the body is a very important "cocking" action. This is especially true for movements in the kip family.

E. *Shoulder Stretching.* Shoulder stretching is especially demanded for two kinds of movements found in gymnastics for girls. The first type belongs to that group of movements requiring a "dislocate" position of the arms. This position is shown in Figure 2-6. You can stretch the muscles involved by holding a stick, such as a broomstick, and then by rotating the stick from the front of your body to the back of your body, you are forced to pass through the "dislocate" position. The grip is taken with the knuckles on top. (Overgrip)

11

Figure 2-5   Figure 2-6

Another type of shoulder stretch can be obtained as shown in Figure 2-7. Remember to use steady, even, pressure. This kind of flexibility will be especially valuable in the performance of movements in the walkover family. The additional arch obtained by this type of flexibility is obvious in Figure 2-8.

2. Strength

Strength is the silent partner of the girl in gymnastics. Even though you will not be performing the dynamic feats of strength, such as "The Iron Cross," that boys love to master, you must develop strength that is less obvious in your particular variety of gymnastics. It is important for you to be aware of certain strength attributes so that the movements that you will be attempting to perform (or spot) will be done with the confidence that comes with adequate strength.

Figure 2-7   Figure 2-8

A. *Tone.* The tone of your muscles will improve with training. Can you feel your muscles tighten? If not, this is a general indication that some effort should be applied to strengthen particular groups of muscles. Please remember that good tone does not imply in any way that you will become more masculine looking. Research scientists in physical education know that the opposite is true.

B. *Grip Strength.* A firm grip is especially demanded for uneven parallel bar work. If your grip is weak, certain movements should not be attempted. Other movements should be spotted carefully if you are not sure of the strength of your grip. The hand of the spotter often can be placed on top of your hand in such cases. The spotter can then feel whether or not you are doing most of the work.

You can get a rough idea of how your grip strength is coming along by gripping a bathroom scale and noting the number of pounds you can squeeze between your hands. Grip strength, as well as other kinds of strength, will improve with the practice of movements in which it is demanded. Squeezing a little rubber ball with the fingers has also been recommended for improving grip strength.

C. *Arms and Shoulders.* Can you "chin" yourself? One "chin" or pull-up is not too much to ask of a girl. How many push-ups can you do? If you can do at least five with your body relatively straight (with slight flexion at the hips), you will probably have sufficient support strength for your work in gymnastics.

One of the better ways to develop these kinds of strength is to let your own body weight do the work for you. If you can't "chin," have someone assist you to the finish position. Then come down to a hang as slowly as you can. To develop push-up strength, start in the "up" position and lower slowly, attempting to keep your body straight, and try to touch your nose to the floor before any other part of your body touches. In the Caslavska sequences you will find the gymnast exhibiting support strength in B-49 to 51; U-9; U-40 to 41 and V-11.

D. *Abdominal ("Tummy") Strength.* Of all of the kinds of "silent" strength you will need in gymnastics, abdominal strength rates very high. Aside from the normal development of this kind of strength while learning uneven bar movements, the sit-up has been most closely identified with the development of abdominal strength.

With a partner it is possible to get a good abdominal workout by following the example in Figure 2-9. You might also try sit-ups in reverse.

Figure 2-9

Try to go down very slowly to your back avoiding the sudden drop which is commonly observed half way down. Try to feel each part of your spine touch the floor as you "curl" down.

E. *Leg Strength.* You will develop leg strength by running, jumping and skipping rope. The vaulting steps recommended for practice in Chapter 3 will also be useful in leg strength development. The trampoline is also recommended as an apparatus for developing leg strength.

In the next chapter you will find that the content has been arranged in a continuing type of preparation for gymnastics. By following the suggested order of movements presented, you will be able to apply the foregoing principles as you learn the basic skills of gymnastics.

3

Gymnastic Skills
Essential For Everyone

In addition to being fun to do, the following sets of fundamentals are the foundation stones for all intermediate and advanced gymnastic work. You should master all of these to be sure that you are ready for more difficult work later on.

As you practice, try out some of the ideas presented in "Gymnastics in 3-D." The last section of this chapter is devoted to this topic. Even as a beginner you will find many things that you are able to do. It will help you to discover and explore gymnastic movements.

ON THE BACK SERIES

Many girls say "I can't" when it comes to gymnastics, but they are usually thinking way over their heads. Lie down on your back, You can certainly do that. While on your back you might kick, squirm, wiggle, roll or balance.

You might tuck, pike or extend (layout) your body. See Figure 3-1. From a sitting position, try to roll back slowly into each of these three positions. Then try to roll faster.

Besides tucking your legs (bending tightly at the knees), there are three things you might do. Your feet may be spread sideways. We call this a *straddle position*. If your feet are in a forward-backward relationship, we call this a *leg stride*. Finally, you might keep your legs together. A combination of leg positions, sometimes called a *stag* or *single leg lever position,* is shown in Figure 3-2. Now try to do your roll-back with different leg positions and combinations.

Figure 3-1   *Figure 3-2*

As your roll-backs get smoother, you'll soon find that you can turn over to your knees thus completing a very primitive form of the backward roll.

Soon after this experience you will be able to perform a back roll from a standing tuck to a standing tuck. See Figure 3-3. A push with the hands (through the arms) is important to the success of this movement. See "C" of Figure 3-3.

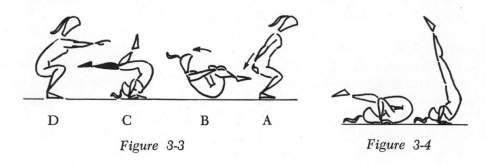

D   C   B   A

Figure 3-3   *Figure 3-4*

Note: the "black" leg represents the proper position for the forward roll.

Getting to your back from your feet can be accomplished in a number of ways. In gymnastics the forward roll is probably the most common way. Essentially, it is the reverse of a back roll but, except as noted in Figure 3-3, beginners often "choke up" when they are asked to go over for the first time. The easiest way to go over is to straddle your legs, place your hands between your feet and simply tip over with your head tucked in. As you go forward, slow down the movement by tensing your arms as they bend.

The "On the Back Series" also includes two important balances. They are important in the early development of the kip which will be discussed later in this chapter. See Figure 3-4. Practice going from one position to the other with straight legs and you may discover the feeling of the kip by yourself.

A balance that will help you with body control while on your back is shown by the little figure in the center of Figure 3-1. Notice that the arms are free. If you can move your legs and still maintain this balance, it will also be helpful later on.

Finally, look at Figure 3-5. This position is known as a "pretzel bend" and is merely an excellent gymnastic stretching exercise. It may take some time and effort in stretching before you look like the little figure but it will pay off eventually in uneven bar work. Don't forget to try some "3-D" on your back by following the suggestions at the end of this chapter.

RUNNING AND GYMNASTICS

Another kind of movement that you have certainly been doing for a long time is running. Running is especially important gymnastically in vaulting, floor exercises and tumbling. Running speed is necessary for a successful vault. You should try to run like a sprinter. Seek the help of a track coach or a physical educator. They have experience in teaching or coaching girls the techniques of running. Girls often have some special problems with their running movements due to hip breadth. As a result, some girls develop a hip sway while running which in turn adds up to lots of lost motion and energy.

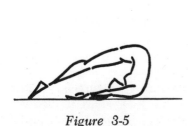

Figure 3-5

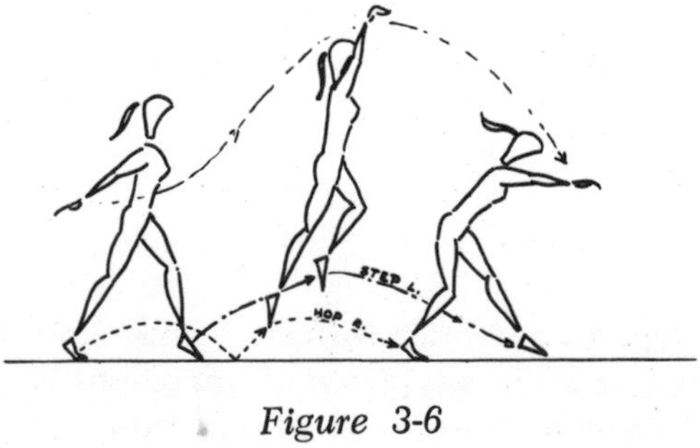

Figure 3-6

Look at Caslavska's run in the vaulting sequence. Her form in V-3 is particularly good. Her run is direct; it has no wasteful side steps nor is it characterized by a hip swing. Her vault was of gold medal calibre because she had a "gold medal" run!

Let us think about two very important movements under this section. They are both movements which the gymnast performs after running. One, the skip step, is particularly a tumbling skill and the other, the hurdle step, is used in tumbling and vaulting.

The skip step is a movement you should master because of its value in many forward and backward tumbling skills. Caslavska uses a skip step no less than six times during her floor exercise. (See Chapter 6)

You see in Figure 3-6 that the skip step is really a hop and a step combined. The little figure is hopping right. You should learn a skip step with a right foot hop, especially if you are right-handed. As you run simply think about hopping on your right foot. Concentrate on the hop. As you hop, stretch out and lift the knee opposite the hopping leg. When you finally step out you may do a roll, a jump with a half turn or simply run and do another skip step. When you can do your skip step with good speed exactly on a spot you select, you will have mastered an important gymnastic skill.

The hurdle step (Figure 3-7) enables you to convert running speed to a two foot take-off used in many kinds of gymnastic jumps. This kind of

Figure 3-7   Figure 3-8

step is used prior to most vaults. The dotted figure in Figure 3-7 is just one of the many kinds of jumps possible. Use the "3-D" chart to discover other possibilities. As in skip steps, you should be able to do the hurdle step exactly where you want to do it. In vaulting, this may require measuring the exact length of your run so the hurdle step can be performed without adjustments in your stride which would break your running form.

Walking, which by now you take for granted, will have an added dimension if you will imitate some of Caslavska's stretch positions every few steps. (See Chapter 6) Stretch on either one or both feet and attempt to hold, but not force, some of the stretch positions you observe in the sequence drawings.

LANDING ON YOUR FEET

As a gymnast, you must become a living spring. "Deadness" is often the term used to describe a person who does not display liveliness in movement. You must develop "more bounce to the ounce."

Little girls often develop a gymnastic bounce quality by jumping rope. Chances are that you have passed this rope skipping age and have put your rope away. Get it out again! Begin to do rope skipping to improve your potential as a gymnast. As you jump, land on your toes and develop a single beat landing (boxer style) instead of the double beat, flat-footed jump you probably used when you were in your rope jumping heyday. By the way, rope jumping is enjoyed by groups of girls who do quite complicated, synchronized work. How about some "3-D" applications of rope jumping? Finally, try to jump rope as silently as possible. When you do, your body will be handling the shock of landing properly in the knees and ankles.

Landing gymnastically requires control and form. In most instances landings are made either at the close of an exercise or in preparation for another movement. Practice jumping down from things. Start low. Progress by landing out of skip steps, hurdle steps and very simple vaults. Jump down from a balance beam or trampoline. Use mats for your landing. Do you make lots of noise when landing? Do you land in control? Caslavska had some difficult landings to make in her Olympic routines. She seldom lost control. In Figure 3-8 you will observe the action which is typical of all gymnastic landings. Notice how the arms assist the lift in the beginning as they swing down, then up. The arms act as balancing weights upon landing. The landing in Figure 3-8 shows the normal path of the arms in a good landing. In this kind of a landing they simply complete their circular sweep. If you have too much forward momentum, the arms may be held back. The opposite is true for landings which are lacking in momentum. In this latter variety, you may fall backward to your hips.

It is therefore important to get the arm weight forward to aid in balance. The shock of landing is absorbed by bending at the ankles and the knees.

THE BACKBENDING SERIES

A gymnast's back is apt to be close to one of two extremes. One kind of back is too loose; the other is too stiff. The ideal gymnastic back has a combination of strength and flexibility. This kind of back is exhibited by gymnastic Olympians. Even in this group, however, variations in back type exist. The back therefore gives us a clue to the type of gymnastic performance we are likely to see.

If you have a good gymnastic back, you will have little difficulty pushing up to the position shown by the center figure of Figure 3-9. The figure on the left could be described as having an acrobatic back. The "stiff back" on the right is typical in many gymnastic beginners. Constant pushing up and stretching in the backbend position is required for the latter.

Figure 3-9

Once you have developed your gymnastic back, three movements will be immediately challenging. They are the backbend from a stand, the kickover and the stand-up from a bridge. These movements are shown in Figure 3-10.

In the backbend, your "tummy" goes in the direction of the arrow. You begin the movement by stretching your head and arms backward. Then you go the rest of the way. A light assist from a friend, immediately above the hips, might be needed on the first few attempts.

The kickover is the "younger sister" of the back walkover. Bending the knee as shown will speed up the movement thus making it easier. Later on you will be able to keep the kicking leg relatively straight. Put the backbend and the kickover together, add a little stretch and voilà! . . . a back walkover.

The stand-up is a little more difficult since it requires just a bit more backbending effort. Once it is mastered, however, the front walkover will be a natural development.

Now apply some "3-D" to this section.

BALANCING

Did you know that you'd be better off on all fours when it comes to balancing? When man decided not to use his hands for transportation and left the four-legged kingdom forever, he created some balancing problems for himself. Although time has healed most of the shock of assuming an erect posture, modern man is still plagued with back problems due to poor posture. Since gymnastic posture requires that we make the most economical use of our body in various positions, it is natural

Figure 3-10   Figure 3-11

to assume that gymnastics contributes to the development of good posture and a pleasing appearance. Balancing activities, and the balance beam in particular, can contribute much to the development of good posture.

In gymnastics we further complicate the balance of man by making it increasingly more difficult to stand. Standing on one hand, for example, offers the ultimate challenge in balance. Rather than list all of the balances in this section, let's look at a few principles of balance. We shall then apply them to the relatively simple head and hand balance (headstand).

1. When a part of you goes one way, something else must go another.
   The old wall problem is an excellent lesson here. Stand with your

heels against any straight wall. Now, touch your toes with your finger tips. What happened? Since your hips could not move backward as you bent forward, you lost balance and fell forward to your hands.

2. Make sure you use the widest possible base appropriate for the balance you select. In gymnastics, the smaller the base of support, the more difficult the balance.

3. Your center of weight (Center of Gravity—C.G.) must remain over the base of support when you are attempting a balance.

4. The higher your center of weight, the more difficult the balance. Compare the difficulty of the two balances shown in Figure 3-11.

Now for our headstand. Look at Figure 3-12 (A, B, C, D and E). In "A" we see the base of support consisting of the hands and head. The ideal arrangement is the tripod. The center of weight is shown in "B," "C," "D" and "E." In each case it is directly over the supporting base. Since the center of weight rises in "B," "C," and "D," we conclude that the highest position ("D") is the most difficult of the three. From "D"

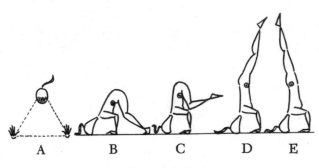

A   B   C   D   E

Figure 3-12

to "E" we see a counter shifting of the hips and feet in order to assume good gymnastic posture or good form. As the hips move forward, the feet move backward. In "E" the body has moved to form a pleasing curve.

THE HAND SUPPORT SERIES

Hand supported movements and holds in modern gymnastics for girls and women are very important. Momentary hand support is commonly demanded while a movement is in progress. Support of any kind is seldom held for more than just a few seconds. Hand support for the purpose of displaying great strength of the arm and shoulders is not an objective for girls. You must simply develop enough strength to keep your arms "locked out" or straight while they support your weight momentarily. For some girls, strengthening the arms will take a little extra time and effort. Handsprings, cartwheels, round-offs and other movements through (not holding) a handstand cannot be done properly without this type of "silent" strength.

Try some hand support skills or movements in "3-D." You will soon find your limit. Finally, you must return to the development of the momentary handstand. It, above all, is the most important hand support or "lock out" skill.

Look at Figure 3-13 (A, B, C, D and E). The figures show the progressive action of the single leg method for developing a handstand. The press-up method commonly used by boys emphasizes strength and is not recommended for beginners. In "A" you will observe the first step. From this position, kick your right (or left) leg up as shown. Feel the levering power of this stretched leg. As you kick you will feel your right

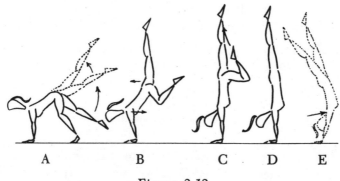

A   B   C   D   E

Figure 3-13

leg pull your body and the bent left leg from the ground. Try to come down slowly placing your weight on the bent leg as you touch the ground or mat.

In "B" the kicking leg has almost reached the handstand position. The arrows show the countering movements of shoulders and hips at this point. Again, lower the foot of the bent leg slowly to the ground. Note that the arms in all sequences are straight ("locked out").

While attempting a handstand, the performer overbalances. Does figure A or B represent an action she should take to avoid falling on her back?

Evaluation Questions

AVOIDING A FALL

Position "C" shows a balanced stand with one knee bent. The balance is easier than the one in "D" because the center of weight is lower due to the bent leg. After many kicks, you will find that you can balance momentarily like the little figure in "C" and once you can, try to stretch the other leg to the regular handstand position shown in "D."

Note the stretched position of the body in "D." A good handstand has only a slight curve. Would you stand on your feet with an extreme arch? Naturally not. The same principle applies to the handstand.

Your real moment of glory will come on the day you get "stuck." That is the day when you kick up and stay there! This will be one of your most thrilling experiences.

A position to avoid is shown in "E." Here it is not so much an arched trunk but the extreme extension at the shoulders which is to be avoided. (See arrow.)

Once the momentary handstand is "old hat," your cartwheels and walkovers will be much improved. You will be prepared for some of the momentary supports that you will experience in vaulting also. More details on hand supports will be found in this chapter under "Casting" and the description of the forward handspring at the end of the chapter on "spotting."

SPLITS AND TIGHT PIKE

While developing your splits and tight pike, you will be experiencing gymnastic pain with a purpose. The development of both these positions will be of immense help later on. A quick glimpse at our Olympic cham-

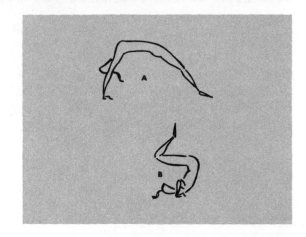

Diagram B:

AVOIDING A FALL

A   B

Figure 3-14

pion in all her events reveals that she uses moving and nonmoving splits at least seventeen times and the tight pike at least six times. For a good example of the latter, look at Figure 48 of the balance beam sequence.

From the time of birth many girls are naturally capable of the splits or tight pike. Particular problems of these girls are discussed elsewhere. For those who are not so blessed, constant stretching is a *must*. If done daily, you will soon acquire the necessary stretching action for the splits and tight pike.

Use the TV commercial method. Pick up the beer or soap commercial you like least and use these blocks of time for stretch practice. For each beer commercial work on your splits; for each soap commercial work on your tight pike. Watch TV in a leotard.

25

In Figure 3-14 (A and B) you will find a sequence recommended for splits practice. Start on one knee as shown. Then slide the other foot forward slowly until pain is evident. Endure the first mild pain you feel for the duration of the commercial and above all, don't bounce. The trunk remains erect. If you have trouble with balance, get someone to steady you or place a chair or table along side of your body. Reverse the position of your legs on your next try. Try to find a surface or situation in which your feet will slide easily.

For the tight pike, there are a number of positions you might try. (See Figure 3-15) To do a pike stretch on your back, while sitting or

Figure 3-15

from a stand, you may need some added pressure since you cannot depend on your body weight alone. Have a friend supply a firm, gentle and even push. Hold the pike with mild pain for half a minute or so.

Try some gymnastics in "3-D" using the splits and tight pike. Go back through the foregoing sections and combine elements from them, too.

THE CASTING SERIES

The cast in any one of its many forms is an important gymnastic cornerstone. It is a "cocking" movement and therefore is commonly used to initiate a second movement.

Figure 3-16 shows a typical bar cast. You should have no special difficulty with this movement. Notice that as the legs swing backward the head and shoulders remain forward so that the direction of the movement is upward rather than backward.

The "supple" movement shown in Figure 3-17 has a subtle cast. It is started by kicking up a single leg from a front support. After the legs are joined, they return together to the floor and the body arches. The weight is then immediately shifted forward and the body explodes upward, piking as it moves. The cast occurs shortly after this point as the legs continue their upward swing and you find that you are almost in a handstand but still moving. Once again the body is piked, the hands leave the ground and you come finally to a stand. If you will practice this movement faithfully you will ultimately achieve the form shown in Figure 3-17. It will be helpful in warming up and it has many carry-over values.

Figure 3-16   Figure 3-17

A cast is also a typical balance beam movement. (See Figure 3-18) In this case the cast is quite mild as casts go. Upon reaching the final position in Figure 3-18, you "roll your own" ending. It might be a dismount. You might lower your knee to the beam. You could tuck up your legs to place your feet on the beam or you might simply lower your body to the astride posture with which you started.

THE KIPPING SERIES

Oh, if only you were a click beetle! Once this little elater is on his back, no other animal, including man, beats him in generating powerful kips. The kip is one of gymnastic's key movements. It sires the head-spring, handspring, back extension roll (back roll through a handstand) and a wide variety of apparatus movements.

"Click" is a good term to remember since it represents very well the explosiveness and quickness of a kip. A kip is never sluggish; it just cannot be done slowly.

The first letter of the word "kip" supplies a clue to the movement. (See Figure 3-19) Every kip contains a stretched and a piked body position. It could be described as a dynamic folding and unfolding of the

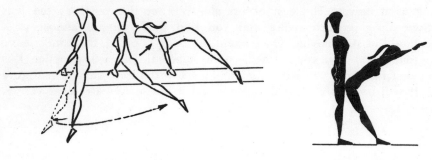

Figure 3-18   Figure 3-19

body. As a matter of fact, the body unfolds so fast that any energy thus produced can be easily transferred to the rest of the body. As a result, the body usually rises in any kipping action.

Your first kip is shown in Figure 3-20. It is actually a kipping action movement which will lend itself to many of the simple finishes that you have been practicing. The kip itself is shown from "C" to "E." Here you can see the folding and unfolding of the body. From "E" you might finish in a bridge, extend very high and roll forward or finish in a handstand and work from there. This latter movement is a bit more advanced, however.

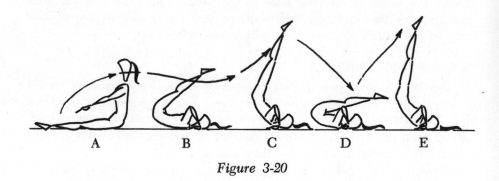

A   B   C   D   E

Figure 3-20

Any soft surface will do during the experimental stage and if you are lucky enough to have the use of a trampoline, you can slow down your kip to get a better "feel" of the movement.

After a kip to a bridge* is easy for you to do, you will find that the neckspring is a good challenge. In such a spring you simply roll forward to position "D" of Figure 3-20 but you will do your kip before the hips are as close to the mats as they are shown to be in the drawing. After this, the kip from the head and hands (headspring) can be attempted. (See Figure 3-21)

Figure 3-21

The kipping action is shown in the black figure of the sequence. Having tilted forward to the off-balance position illustrated, the piked legs are rapidly kipped to the position shown by the dotted figure. This movement need not end in a stand at first. You may simply finish in a bridge. If your backbending work is progressing well, the finished stand will not be very difficult.

For your first apparatus kip, seek out a set of even parallel bars (used by the boys) and set the rails a little below shoulder height. A very elementary kip can be done on these bars. If you are successful, it will not be long before you can do some of the uneven bar kips which are more advanced.

Look at Figure 3-22. After jumping to a piked inverted hang position ("A" to "B") you "ride" forward in this position to "D." You then "ride" back to a position similar to "B" shown as the figure in black. The kip is done at the very end of this backward swing and it is not difficult if your body swings properly as shown. Having kipped, you finish in a

---

*A "bridge" is a term commonly applied to the end position of a backbend.

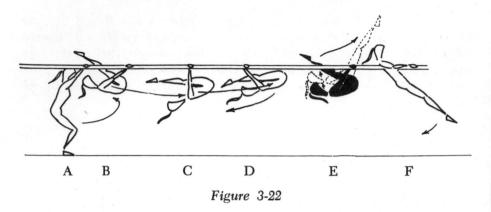

<table>
<tr><td>A</td><td>B</td><td>C</td><td>D</td><td>E</td><td>F</td></tr>
</table>

Figure 3-22

position known as an upper arm hang ("F"). Shortly after this your feet will touch down on the mats since the bars are lower than usual.

As you work with this kip it is important for you to feel two definite "bounces" in the piked inverted hang-swing. (B to D and D to B) The "bounces" occur at each end of the pendulum swing, one at the forward end and one at the backward end. The kipping action coincides with the rear "bounce." You must wait for the "bounce" before you kip. Keep your arms straight.

Practice the piked swing without kipping. Feel the "bounces." Once you do, you will be ready for some work on advanced kips on the uneven parallel bars. Work hard on this basic kipping work. Once you master it, you'll be one up on the little click beetle. You'll know where you're going; he doesn't!

ELEMENTARY BAR SERIES

To help you to get familiar with the uneven parallel bars, there are some elementary, yet key, movements to learn. Mastering these movements will make your first attempts on the unevens much more diversified. You may do some of your practicing on any low horizontal bar. Even at the more advanced level it is not imperative that you have a real set of unevens to work on. If they are available, however, use them.

The first of these key movements is called a single knee-up. (See Figure 3-23) Get into the single knee hang shown in "A." As soon as you are set, learn to swing suspended from the knee and hands keeping your arms stretched.

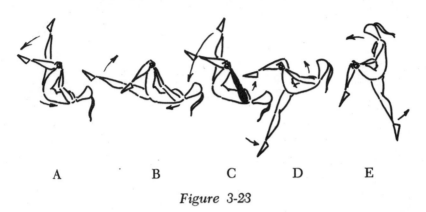

A   B   C   D   E

Figure 3-23

You will use your free leg to start the swing. You need only to kick gently to begin a rhythmic pendulum swing. When you "feel" a good, stretched swing, you are ready to do the knee-up. Raise your free leg as shown in "C" in preparation for an extra strong kick. Note the straight arms which are shown in black on the little figure.

In "D" the kick is in its final stages and the body rotates upward. At this point you pull in towards the bar before your kick loses its punch. Your weight comes closer to the bar; therefore you move faster.

In "E" the little figure is almost up in support. She continues to pull in towards the bar to arrive in a stride (sometimes called split) support. Once you master the knee-up, you can try it by dropping back from a stride support. The single knee circle forward will also be a natural development. (See Figure 4-2, Chapter 4) Once you have learned a single knee circle, the more difficult Mill circle will develop nicely. In a Mill circle, both legs remain extended.

The hip pullover, shown in Figure 3-24, is another basic bar circle. This time, however, the direction of the circle is backward. To succeed in the hip pullover, you will need to combine elements of strength and coordination. You will need to have enough bent-arm strength to hold your weight momentarily in the position shown in "C." Generally speaking, if you can "chin" yourself once on a bar, you should have adequate strength.

A well coordinated hip pullover does not require chinning strength, however. Most girls will rely on strength during the learning period and then find out for themselves that with proper coordination the movement is much easier. The coordination involves a simultaneous kick and pull.

31

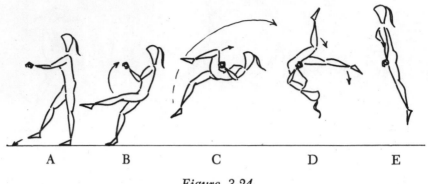

Figure 3-24

If you kick but fail to pull you will be unsuccessful. The reverse is also true. When you first attempt a hip pullover, it will be helpful to take turns with a friend. Your friend can help you by placing her hand under the bent leg in "C." As you begin to move, she will then lift this leg rapidly. You will soon be kicking over the bar without help. To complete the movement you should attempt to stop in a front support on the bar as shown in "E." Later you will do the hip pullover without bending the knee so noticeably.

The early performance of a hip pullover is an excellent way to learn the "feel" of a hip circle backward. In a hip circle you cast from a front support and travel one full circle around the bar. As in the pullover, it is necessary to keep your hips as close to the bar as you can. Both movements are completed in the same way but the hip circle backward is faster; therefore you may have a little more difficulty stopping in a front support.

The push-off, swing and feint, shown in Figure 3-25, must be done on a regular set of uneven parallel bars. If you have never had an opportunity to perform on the unevens, do a little exploring before you try any movements involving both bars.

"Crawling around the bars" will be helpful. At this stage you will simply get up on the bars and explore many positions. You can try to do any of the things you have already mastered on the low bar. You should also try a front support on the high bar to rid yourself of a natural fear of the height involved. Turning over the high bar from a front support will help you get used to the height of the upper bar. In short,

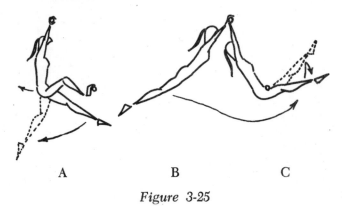

A   B   C

Figure 3-25

do as many different kinds of things as you can. Then, when you run out of ideas, try the push-off, swing and feint.

The feint or "fake wrap-around," as it is sometimes called, is often used by girls to check on the height of the low bar to see if it is adjusted in a position which is most comfortable for their size. It could be called a measurement movement. Taller girls will perform with the low bar a bit lower or wider than shorter girls who will make an adjustment in an opposite direction. In competitive routines at the intermediate or advanced level the adjustment is necessary for variations of the wrap-around movement. A wrap-around is a term applied to a hip circle backward on the low bar without the use of the hands. During the movement the gymnast travels from a long hang on the high bar to a support on the low bar.

The feint is an important movement for you, the beginner, as well. It enables you to swing in a long hang; it provides a little coordination challenge and it is excellent preparation for the wrap-around.

In "A" (Figure 3-25) you will observe the push-off. Notice the straight arms. The free leg swings backward as the foot pushes off. Pushing with the foot as the leg swings backward is the coordination phase of the movement. In "B" the little figure has arrived in a long hang. The swing forward should be strong enough to bring your "belt line" into the low bar with medium speed. Try to hit the bar in a layout position. If you pike too soon, there is a chance that the bony, unprotected parts of your hips will be bruised. For this reason a beach towel is sometimes wound around the low bar for first attempts at the feint.

As soon as contact is made just above the hips, the body bends and the stretched legs continue to circle upward around the low bar. You literally wrap your body around the bar; hence the name "wrap-around." The word "feint" is used to describe the movement since you will not actually complete the hip circle. As your legs reach the point where they no longer will circle backward, they come down again circling in the opposite direction. Finally, you finish the feint in a long hang. From the long hang, you have a number of options. You can drop off at the end of the backward swing. You can raise your legs prior to the end of the backward swing to arrive at a rear support-hang on the low bar on the next forward swing. You might skin-the-cat on the high bar. Finally, don't forget that you will have learned a very commonly used measurement movement. The wrap-around itself should be a fairly easy goal after the preparation of the feint.

When you become a gymnastic intermediate, you will find other ways to get into a swing in the long hang position. One of these is a cast to a long hang from a front support on the high bar. In another, you sit on the low bar facing the high bar and cast off the low bar with a half turn to a long hang. These two movements should be done with close supervision, however. Don't try them on your own without help. Your grip strength may not be adequate and you could have a nasty fall.

ON THE BEAM

Although you can practice much of your early beam work on a four inch stripe on the floor, you will eventually have to get up on the real thing. A piece of lumber, commonly known as a two-by-four, can be placed on the floor in such a way that the four inch side is up. With such a simple and inexpensive "beam" you can become familiar with the balance necessary for work on a regular beam.

Many wonderful dads, and especially those dads who are handy with tools, have built homemade beams for their budding gymnasts. A former world champion on the beam, Eva Bosakova of Czechoslovakia, recalled the role of her dad and her first attempts at balance beam exercises.

> My father always prescribed thirty minutes of work on the beam during which it was necessary to remain on this apparatus, constantly in action; walking, hopping, turning and again walking without rest.

Almost all of the basic floor movements can be attempted on the beam. Should your early experience be restricted only to the advice of

Bosakova, your confidence and form would be likely to show great improvement.

Other than variations of the cast which are commonly performed on the beam, most of your work will consist of adapted floor work. When such movements are attempted on the small surface provided, they become significantly more difficult. The cartwheel and forward roll are no longer elementary in nature when they are performed on the beam. They become controlled and skillfully executed, advanced movements.

Try walking first. Instead of the normal, earthbound style, where your feet point directly ahead your leg will turn out so that your foot can be placed diagonally across the beam. This will feel awkward at first but due to better grip and control you will soon prefer this style.

Erect posture is also a requirement. When you stretch out there is less chance of losing control since your body will be united to form fewer levers than if you were to perform without adequate tension in the muscles. The stiffness that is very often observed in a beginner on the beam will eventually disappear. This will be replaced by movement grace and control which in turn will make a valuable contribution to your posture and appearance both on the beam and off. Here then is another bonus of gymnastics.

While on the beam, keep your eyes focused ahead of you. Try to avoid looking down. Remember, the beam isn't going anywhere; you are! A prominent English coach (with an American movie star's name), June Allison, recommends the practice of "looking down your nose" as you extend your trunk. Try this technique while you observe yourself in a mirror.

As a beginner you should also master:
1. Lying down on the beam (front and back).
2. Dance steps such as the waltz and polka. You might even try the "twist." Some of the Olympians in Tokyo did "twist-like" movements in their routines.
3. Sitting movements with the "3-D" approach.
4. Turns of all kinds. The pivot turn is shown in Figure 3-26. As your arms swing upward you rise to your toes and turn immediately. As you complete 180 degrees (one-half turn) your heels return to the beam. Other turns may be practiced on the floor or two-by-four experimentally. Finally, you will attempt these turns on the beam itself.
5. Look back through this chapter for ideas about getting on (mounting) and getting off (dismounting) the beam.

Figure 3-26   Figure 3-27

6. Simple jumps and hops on the beam. Place little boxes on your two-by-four and try to get over these in various ways. Later, try soft objects of various shapes and sizes on a regulation beam.
7. Try a scale, See Figure 3-27. The important objective in a scale aside from balance will be your ability to lift your leg without bending forward at the hips.

GYMNASTICS IN 3-D

The gymnastic movement cube, shown in Figure 3-28 is presented to you as a source of ideas for gymnastic movement exploration. The little figures surrounding the cube are simply examples of some of the possibilities. If you were to attempt to do all of the movements or positions you could easily list more than 600. Combining ideas will present an infinite variety.

The three sides of the cube in the diagram represent three dimensions of gymnastic movement. The front side represents fundamental body positions such as sitting, standing, leaping in the air and others. Starting with positions on the back where there is a wide base of support, you can progress to positions with no base or those in which the body leaves the ground.

On the top side of the cube arm position variations of the tuck, pike and layout are suggested. On the side of the cube, you will find suggestions for varied leg positions.

A movement in one dimension would simply be, for example, exploring a variety of things you might do on your back. The little figure under the cube just happens to be on her back in a layout position with her

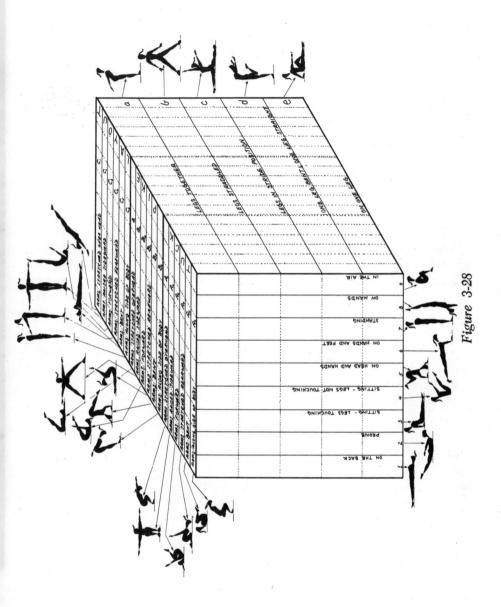

Figure 3-28

37

How many combinations on the "3-D" chart, page 37, have you mastered? Beginners can easily perform 100 combinations.

Evaluation Questions

arms along side her body. Utilizing the concept of the cube, and having just this much information we could say she is two dimensional since she is not only on her back but is also in a layout with her arms alongside her body. Since she has her legs together, she also satisfies a requirement on the side of the cube ("a"—Legs Together). We might refer to her position by using the following shorthand . . . *1-C6-a*. Now she is three dimensional.

Let's consider 5-B5-b. In the first dimension you are on head and hands. Adding the second dimension (B5) you will also pike with your arms bent. Other arm positions will be extremely difficult in this dimension, if not impossible. In some positions you therefore might be able to apply only a two dimensional suggestion. The third dimension (b) is the suggestion to straddle your legs. If you are successful, you will have done a pike straddle head and hand balance.

Finding positions is only half the work, however. By the time you have mastered many of the movements suggested in this chapter you should think of ways to use the cube in combination with these movements. For example, how many things can you do at the end of a skip step? Having done some of the movements after your skip step you might ask, "How can I get out of this movement gracefully?" By combining two positions or two movements with interesting connecting movements, you will at last be performing a gymnastic exercise rather than simply performing and isolated stunt.

The little figures surrounding the cube are not moving; or are they? Look again. Think of them as action ideas, not simply positions. Are they moving backward, forward or sideward? That is also something you must decide. Are they turning or twisting?

You might keep a record of combinations you have tried by the shorthand method suggested. Gymnastic experts have been looking for a simple way to record gymnastic movements for quite some time. This shorthand method may not be the best method but it *is* a method. Some earlier classic gymnastic works had such complicated descriptions for movement that it took a great deal of concentration to decipher and understand what the author had in mind.

CONCLUSION

Once you have become fairly competent in all of the essential skill areas of gymnastics, you truly will be a gymnast. Any gymnastic club and certainly the gymnastic coach will welcome you with open arms. Seek the leadership of a woman's coach if possible.

We men have our limitations in gymnastics for girls and women. Competitively we can become too severe and demanding; most of us know very little about ballet or modern dance and we can't always discuss your personal problems.

Each year we see the emergence of more and more competent female instructors in gymnastics in the United States. We men can help. We are especially helpful in spotting. In the final analysis, however, a woman's touch will make your gymnastic experience and participation something that we men, coaches, non-coaches, teachers and spectators, can really appreciate and admire. We'll be apt to say, "If I were a girl, I'd do gymnastics."

Spotting — The Detective Work of Gymnastics

Spotting is the term applied to the active help a gymnast receives while performing or while learning new gymnastic movements. Spotting goes one step beyond the preparatory level of gymnastics. You may have an ideal gymnastic body in terms of strength and flexibility and you may be knowledgeable in gymnastics, but this will not automatically mean that you will immediately be able to learn all kinds of gymnastic movements.

The two main deterrents in acquiring gymnastic skill are lack of coordination and fear. These elements are painfully apparent especially after the requirements of gymnastic preparation have been fully met and beginning skills have been mastered. Fear is always a detrimental factor in any human performance. Ability in coordination seems to vary from person to person.

A coordinated movement is one in which you successfully harmonize appropriate parts of your body in seemingly effortless action. Even though a movement may be rated "difficult," a good performer may tell you that it is easy to do. We conclude that a well coordinated performance does indeed make that movement easier.

As a spotter, you must be aware of the timing, explosiveness and rhythm of a movement. Your detective work begins with an understanding of the coordination required for a movement. If you attempt to spot a performer without such understanding you may do more harm than good.

COORDINATION

The outline which follows is presented to familiarize you with clues you might obtain for spotting and performing gymnastic movements. They all relate in some way to coordination.

1. *Start on the Floor.*

   a. How many familiar movements are contained within the movement that you have selected to learn or spot? It's rather like playing the old parlor game, "What's in a word?" In this game you attempt to find as many words as possible which can be spelled with letters contained in the word selected. Make a list of the movements you uncover using this technique.

   b. Can you perform all of the easier movements which are relatives of the one you have selected? If not, these should be mastered first.

   c. Can you do a movement on the floor which is similar to the apparatus movement you have selected? Start with the floor every chance you get. Almost every apparatus movement has at least a second cousin on the floor. Since the floor is always available, you may be able to double your practice of the movement and also learn to simplify spotting procedures.

2. *Rhythm.* Can you identify the rhythm of a movement? Rhythm is to music what coordination is to movement. All body parts work in movement harmony when coordination is present just as an excellent conductor unites the abilities of many musicians to perform a symphony.

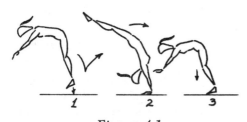

Figure 4-1

For example, in the combination of a roundoff and a back handspring (See Caslavska sequences listed under appropriate headings in the Index in Chapter 6), you should hear three distinct beats starting with the landing in the roundoff and ending with the landing in the back handspring. In Figure 4-1 you see how the feet, hands, feet action of this combination could be heard as three rhythmic beats (1, 2, 3) each having an equal value in terms of time and intensity. In a poor performance, one often may hear a strong single beat ("1") followed by a pause and then two beats of equal value ("2," "3"). The trouble is poor coordination which results in the incorrect rhythm. You may thus hear this clue to a poor performance. "The operation was successful, but the patient died." The missing ingredient, "life," is rhythm Through rhythm, movement takes on the characteristic of elegance . . . of beauty.

Your body sings a silent song of rhythm. In watching or imagining a movement you have selected to learn, make vocal sounds or tap out sounds which correspond to the movement. After repeating this procedure many times, try to imagine the sound combined with a mental image of the movement. This will serve as a clue to performance later on when the actual sounds of movement can be heard. Learning the rhythm of movement will help you to become a good spotter as well as a good performer. Your hands will move and assist the performer much as the orchestra leader coordinates his hand movements and occasionally his whole body in the rhythm of the music he conducts.

3. *Pantomime.* A pantomimed movement is one in which certain parts of a movement or the entire movement are simulated in ways which will often differ somewhat from the actual movement itself.

   a. See if it is possible to lift or be lifted through a slow version of the movement.

   b. By using some item of hand apparatus, such as a stick, see if a simulated performance can be done.

   c. Can the movement be simulated in the water? Many movements, dangerous for the novice on the floor or apparatus, can be safely simulated in water. In the water, the movement is done slowly which in turn can lead to the mastery of the coordination involved.

   d. Pantomime the movement on the relatively safe surface of the trampoline.

   e. Pantomime the movement on the floor. For example, the rhythm of a cartwheel is 1, 2, 3, 4. During the cartwheel, one may observe the sequence, hand, hand, foot, foot as the movement progresses. To pantomime a cartwheel, simply place the hands and feet on the floor in the correct order and with the correct rhythm as the stunt itself would require. You proceed by placing the hands and feet appropriately even though the movement you do is a far cry from a cartwheel.

4. *Progression.* Let us think of progression as whole movement parts of the movement you have selected to learn or spot. You could not create a cake by baking each of its ingredients separately. On the other hand, when you were a little girl your mother probably had you start out with very simple baking chores. Perhaps she let you roll a bit of dough that was yours to bake (and eat!). Your pride in that baked crust was as important to you as the new creation of an

epicurean. So it is with movement. The crust is a whole part of the pie but the whole pie will come later.

We have really touched upon this subject in the foregoing but it will do no harm to repeat the thought that all movements can be broken down into whole movements which are similar to them but not as advanced. Such movements are all related to a single gymnastic movement family. When we learn them in order from the easiest to the most difficult we have applied the principle of progression. Try some mental gymnastics and see if you can select ten or more movements which could be called a progression for a forward roll.

5. *Explosiveness.* Explosiveness is the speed factor of coordination. Without explosiveness, a movement may become so sluggish as to make it impossible to perform. Does the movement you have selected need to be done rapidly? If so, where and how can speed be added by the performer or the spotter? Should the run be faster? Is strength lacking? Is flexibility lacking?

a. How might the performer be turned faster?

b. Is greater running speed required?

c. Are the arms or legs swinging, kicking or flinging fast enough?

d. Is a tighter tuck, pike or stretch needed?

e. What kind of strength semes to be lacking?

f. Is the performer too loose causing her to act like a "Rag Doll"?

FEAR

Fear is the friendly enemy of the gymnast. It is friendly in the sense that it may very well prevent you from foolishly destroying yourself. Fear is an enemy of movement, however. You will not be able to perform correctly when it is present in any abnormal degree.

Once you hesitate in fear, your body often responds in nonperformance. The suggestions which follow must be attacked creatively. In this way you may overcome most fears by eliminating their causes. Once the fear subsides to a healthy variety, you will have completed most of your detective work.

1. *Eliminate Height.*

a. Can the movement be performed at a lower height?

b. If the movement selected is to be performed on apparatus can this movement or a movement very similar to it be performed on the floor?

c. Is it possible to set up a platform of some type so that the movement will end on the platform rather than a lower level? Some typical arrangements are seen in Figure 4-2.

d. Can the spotter do her work from a higher position by standing on a platform or some other apparatus? Sometimes fear is eliminated simply due to the closeness of the spotter.

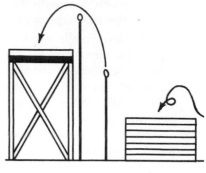

Figure 4-2

2. *Hand Spotting.* It will be helpful to review the principles of mechanics which are outlined in Chapter 2.

   a. Determine the critical point of the movement. Movies and sequence photographs are helpful.

      (1) In circles moving towards the floor, the critical point is at the bottom of the circle. Spotting is planned for this critical point.

      (2) In most tumbling movements the critical point is usually associated with the principle which dictates that a high C.G. is desirable.

      (3) Movements requiring a hand grip should be spotted so that the gymnast knows that if she lets go she will be fully protected.

      (4) Are the head and neck involved in any danger?

      (5) In any jump or vault where the gymnast is above the spotter, the spotter should reach as high as is convenient so that early contact can be made.

   b. The spotter should be in a position which will be of greatest benefit to the performer without in any way hindering the performer's movement.

   c. Both the gymnast and the spotter should understand the planned action of the spotter.

   d. The spotter should be sure that her own hands are protected in planning the spot. Sometimes the spotter faces a greater danger than the performer.

   e. Practice hand spotting forward rolls, cartwheels, backbends and handsprings. Spotting is a skill which is essential for a developing gymnast. By learning to spot simple movements, you prepare yourself progressively for more difficult and complicated spotting. You might even attempt to spot movements you know in advance will be well done. In this manner you can test your timing and you will know whether or not you can actually get your hands on the performer.

f. Verbal directions, if needed, should be short and to the point. These directions are usually associated with the critical point of the movement. After the performance of a movement, ask your partner what she thought was wrong.

3. *How Can a Landing Be Made Softer?*
    a. Additional mats?
    b. Foam rubber scraps?
    c. Use the trampoline?
    e. Perform from land to water. If you elect to do a movement at poolside, make sure there is no danger of slipping and hitting the side.
    f. Use sawdust pits or jumping pits?
    g. Have the performer supported by a belt or some other rigging?

4. *Belt Spotting.* Because of its technical nature and due to many possible misapplications, belt spotting should be used only as a last resort. Although the gymnast is usually secure, she may not get the natural "feel" of the movement. Only a qualified person should help with advanced belt spotting. Spotting with a twisting belt and an overhead rigging is an art in itself and is a must for advanced movements on the trampoline.

5. *Standard Equipment Adapted for Spotting.*
    a. Dismounts to the surface of a trampoline. Always think of ways to use this excellent apparatus for spotting and learning.
    b. Stand on apparatus to raise your level for the spot.
    c. Use an adjustable wall bar (horizontal bar) for uneven bar movements.
    d. Use a ramp arrangement by placing a mat on a standard springboard. Movements can then be performed down hill and in many instances they will be easier to spot and perform with such an arrangement.
    e. Use a standard 2″ x 4″ for lead-up beam work and for spotting certain movements on the beam.

6. *Homemade Spotting Aids.*
    a. Towels rolled lengthwise and wrapped with tape.

   b. Two towels prepared as in "a" are used as a substitute belt. One is placed in front and one is placed in back of the gymnast. The ends of the towels are then twisted and held by two spotters, one on each side.

   c. Strips of cellular (foam) matting are useful. A width of four inches will be an excellent balance beam aid since it will eliminate most of the pain associated with learning the forward and backward rolls on the beam.

   d. A canvas or "duck" net can be made (5′ x 9′). Six handles are sewn securely to each of the long sides. A cotton blanket can be attached with snaps. The net can be used by groups of seven; one performer and six supporters. The net is used to catch the gymnast in a wide variety of movements.

   e. Rolled mats or a pile of the new flat-fold mats make excellent spotting devices and platforms of various kinds.

The following outline is a summation of many of the points contained in this chapter and those of Chapter 2. This outline may be used in your gymnastic detective work. Having selected a stunt or movement, go over each point of the outline to obtain clues about learning or spotting procedures which will be helpful. Following the outline we will attack one movement, the handspring forward, as an example of the application of the outline to a specific problem.

A CHECK LIST FOR SPOTTING AND LEARNING GYMNASTIC MOVEMENTS

I. Do you understand the movement?
  A. What is it called; what does it look like?
  B. What is the gymnastic category of the movement?
    1. Is it in the rotational (circle or arc) group?
      a. Is it a swing?
        (1) In a hang?
        (2) In a support?
      b. Circle with vertical path on a bar?
      c. Other circles on apparatus?
      d. An aerial circle (somersault)?
      e. Circle on floor with path parallel to floor?
      f. Circle with vertical path done on the floor?
      g. A cast?
      h. A kip?
    2. Is it a balance?
    3. Is it in the flexibility group?
      a. A split?
      b. Is backbending involved?

   c. Is there a hamstring stretch?
   d. Is shoulder flexibility needed?
   e. Is it a side-bending movement?
  4. Is it in the vaulting group?
  5. Is it in the strength group?
   a. Support?
   b. Grip?
   c. Abdominal?
   d. Arm?
   e. Leg?
 C. What mechanical principles are involved?
  1. Is the C.G. a factor?
   a. C.G. in bar circle?
   b. C.G. in circle parallel to ground?
   c. C.G. in balancing?
   d. Will it be helpful to spot near the C.G.?
  2. Are Newton's three laws involved?
   a. Law of Inertia?
   b. Law of Acceleration?
   c. Law of Action-Reaction?
  3. Is a lever or moment involved?
  4. Does a body axis play a part in the movement?

II. What is the role of flexibility in the movement?

III. What kind of strength is involved?

IV. How is the movement coordinated?
 A. Can the coordination be learned on the floor?
  1. Are there familiar movements contained in it?
  2. Should an easier movement be mastered first?
  3. If on apparatus, can a similar movement be done on the floor?
 B. What is the rhythm of the movement?
  1. What are its sounds?
  2. Can you visualize it?
 C. Can the movement be pantomimed?
  1. Can you be lifted through it?
  2. Can it be simulated with a stick or other object?
  3. Can it be done in water?
  4. Can it be simulated on the trampoline?
 D. What are the lead-ups or progression?
 E. Is there an explosive quality?

V. Is the performer afraid? Why?
 A. Should height be eliminated?
 B. What kind of hand spotting (if any)?
  1. What is the critical or dangerous point?
   a. Bottom of a verticle circle?
   b. Does C.G. need to be high?

      c. Is loss of grip possible?
      d. Are head and neck in danger?
      e. Is a jump or vault involved?
  2. What is the position of the spotter?
  3. Does the gymnast understand the spotting action?
  4. Is the spotter in danger?
  5. Should some easier movements be spotted first?
  6. Are any verbal directions needed?

C. How can a landing be made softer?
  1. Additional mats?
  2. Foam rubber scraps?
  3. Trampoline?
  4. Perform into water?
  5. Pits?

  6. Belt support or other rigging?

D. Should movement be done in a belt?

E. Can standard equipment be used?

F. What homemade spotting device could be made?

PUTTING THE CHECK LIST TO USE (The Handspring Forward)

Using the foregoing check list, let's analyze the learning and spotting problems of a forward handspring. We will refer below to the sequence (A, B, C. and D) found in Figure 4-3.

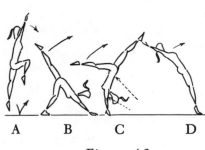

An additional reference is the sequence F(59-63) of Caslavska's floor exercise. In this sequence she does a variation of the handspring.

The handspring belongs to the rotational group. It contains a kip element as seen in C to D of the diagram. You will also recognize the presence of the following elements which are of a lesser importance:

A   B   C   D

Figure 4-3

1. Backbending of a dynamic variety (D)
2. Splitting of the legs (C)
3. Hamstring stretch (B)
4. Push-off strength of arms and shoulders (C)

The handspring is also in the vaulting group. It is really a vault over floor space. The body is in the air between C and D.

As in all tumbling movements, a high center of gravity (C.G.) will be helpful as you perform a handspring. Further, if a spotter can help you by lifting at the correct time, you will be assured of a high center of gravity during the learning stages.

The strength factor in this movement involves the arms and shoulders. Your handspring will be higher if you are able to push off with the hands as shown in C.

Some of the easier, related movements found within the handspring are:

1. A momentary handstand
2. A skip step
3. Ability to perform a two-foot landing
4. Moving splits
5. Handstand limber over to a backbend (In this movement, the weight is simply displaced forward from the handstand, and you drop to your feet without removing your hands from the floor.)
6. Simple kipping action (See Chapter 3)

The rhythm is similar to . . .

da——da——————bip——————————————boom

The "da——da" represents the final portion of the skip step followed in short order by the hand placement (bip) and after push-off and flight the landing on the feet (boom).

The handspring action can be simulated on the trampoline. You will especially feel the action-reaction of the push-off phase which is difficult to feel on the mats or the floor. You will need a soft landing surface during the learning phase.

The explosive part of the movement is the kipping action of the right leg (C to D). The right leg "explodes" to catch up with the left leg which leads the movement.

Since your first attempts to perform a forward handspring might result in some unpleasant landings, it is important that you and your friends learn to spot the movement properly. Before any attempts are made, you should be well along in the performance of the easier, related movements already mentioned and possibly the headspring which is described in Chapter 3.

In spotting, a high C.G. can be maintained in the following ways:

1. By keeping your arms straight.

2. By keeping your head back. If you lower your head (chin on chest position), you will naturally round your back and thus lower your C.G. In Figure 4-4 you may observe and compare the faults mentioned with the correct position and also note what happens to the C.G.

Figure 4-4

3. By having spotters, one on each side, place their hands at two points on each side of the performers as shown by the dotted arrows in C of Figure 4-3. This is the critical moment. At this time you are kicking and pushing. Spotting efforts at this time will be easier since they are applied to a movement already in progress. The spotters should stay with you by keeping their hands in contact with your body until you come to a stand. You practice the spotting skill by attempting to get your hands to the proper place and in the proper position while a skilled performer does the handspring. You may also spot the handstand limber to a bridge. The same procedure is used but speed is not a factor.

4. By performing the handspring from a raised surface to a lower one or by practicing the skill by performing it "down hill" on a ramp arrangement. In either arrangement you will add important inches to the center of gravity.

By applying the check list, we have solved or at least have obtained important clues for performing or spotting a handspring forward. Seek the guidance of an experienced teacher or coach. Get help. Don't take foolish chances!

The Language
of Gymnastics

The language of gymnastics is complicated and very confusing. Although some countries have worked out a fairly consistent nomenclature, such has not been the case in English speaking countries. In addition, gymnasts in the United States are confronted with gymnastic terms derived from many foreign languages. We have adopted mostly German and French terms to describe certain movements. Kehre in German for example means "a turn." The Germans qualify the kind of turn by adding a prefix such as "stütze" meaning support. The full term, "stütze-kehre," is therefore a turn from support. We have further complicated these terms so that "kehre" to us may mean a very selective kind of turn and "stütze" may mean (to us) a particular movement not understood by the Germans who originally gave us the word.

The world of gymnastic language is also replete with terminology which honors a particular gymnast who is credited with the first notable performance of a movement. Unless you know exactly what the movement is, a foreign dictionary will not give a clue. A very popular side horse movement, a Moore, was named in honor of Roy E. Moore. Moore was very instrumental in the development of gymnastic programs in the United States and one of few Americans to have a popular gymnastic term bear his name. Only one woman has been so honored; her name is used more than any other to describe an uneven bar movement similar to a "skin-the-cat." She is Larisa Latynina of Russia. To do a "Latynina," (see Figure 5-1) you turn your body through your arms while hanging from the high bar facing away from the low bar. Instead of turning all the way to a hang, you hook your toes on the low bar, release one of your hands, and arrive on the low bar in a seat or stand facing one of the ends of the apparatus. This movement is probably one of the easiest ones that bears the name of a famous gymnast.

A more recent complication for girls and women has been the wide use of ballet terms in gymnastics. All of these terms are in French and give a fairly accurate description of the movements. But you must know French and more than that you should actually see descriptions of the movements themselves. At least two authors have given special treatment to ballet for gymnastics.[2,3] One of these authors, Grace Kaywell, has also assisted in the development of a special set of long playing records for gymnastic ballet.[4]

Several attempts have been made to standardize the language of gymnastics but these have never received wide support or been popular. At the turn of the century, the YMCA of North America published several little books covering the full range of gymnastics. One of the last editions was published in 1919 and is very rarely seen today.

An excellent condensation of terminology appeared in 1930. It was written by one of the pioneers of gymnastics in the United States, Dr. Leopold Zwarg. Much of the terminology mentioned by Dr. Zwarg is in use today. Let's take a look at some of the major categories which apply to gymnastics for girls and women.

GYMNASTIC TERMINOLOGY IN A NUTSHELL

Hangs, Stands, Supports and Seats. There is often a combination of a hang and a stand, a support and a stand, a hang and a lying position, or a support and a lying position. Whenever you get into one of these positions you find yourself in either a *cross* or *side* relation to the apparatus.

Look at Figure 5-2. The drawing shows the breadth axis and length axis of the body. The term "cross" is used when the breadth axis of the gymnast is at right angles to the length axis of the apparatus. The term "side" is used when the breadth axis of the body is parallel with the length axis of the apparatus.

A cross or side position occurs in three possible ways:

1. Frontways—Gymnast faces apparatus

---

[2]Prchal, Mildred, *Artistic Gymnastics—Floor Exercises*. Berwyn, Ill.: The Author (2419 Scoville Ave. 60402), 1964.

[3]Kaywell, Grace, *Ballet for Gymnastics*. Los Angeles: Sundby Publications (410 Broadway, Santa Monica, Cal.), 1965.

[4]*Ballet for Gymnastics* (3 L.P. records) by Grace Kaywell. Stepping Tones Record Co., P.O. Box 64334, Los Angeles, Cal.

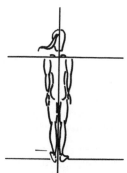

Figure 5-1   *Figure 5-2*

2. Rearways—Gymnast's back is towards apparatus
3. Sideways—Side of gymnast is towards apparatus

The diagram in Figure 5-3 shows a variety of standing positions at the uneven parallel bars. The arrows show the direction the gymnast is facing. The bar nearest the top of the page represents the high bar. Can you name the positions? Since they are all stands, they are either cross-stands or side-stands. The position at the extreme right is a side-stand right sideways, often shortened to side stand R. To make the terms completely correct you might even tell the location of the gymnast with respect to the end or section of the apparatus. You might read, "From a side-stand facing the left third of the beam . . . ." Remember that these terms also apply to hangs, supports and seats.

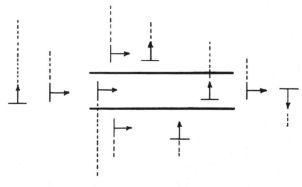

Figure 5-3

Were there such a stunt as a "Caslavska" (there is none we know about) what gymnastic movement would merit the name?

Common Positions.

1. Hangs. In a hang the body usually is suspended by the hands but frequently some other part of the body is the point of suspension. We see elbow hangs, upper arm hangs, knee hangs (hock hangs), inverted hangs (upside down) and squat hangs.

2. Supports. In a support, the body is suspended from the shoulders. In a free support the entire weight is carried by the arms. In most supports the body may lean well over the apparatus thus removing a portion of the weight from the arms. These positions are sometimes called rests.

3. Stands. Stands are found on the apparatus as well as the floor. There are straight stands, pike stands, squat stands, knee stands, straddle stands (feet apart parallel to breadth axis with no bend at the knees), shoulder stands, headstands and handstands.

4. Hang-Lying Positions. The gymnast in such a position is partly hanging and partly lying but most of the weight is suspended from the hands.

5. Support-Lying Positions. In this kind of position the gymnast is partly supporting herself and partly lying but most of the weight is supported by the arms.

6. Seats. According to their axis relation, seats are called cross seats or side seats. If the legs straddle the apparatus the position might be called a straddle seat. Cross seats are seen more frequently on the uneven bars and on the beam than side seats. On the uneven bars the cross seats may be termed "inner" or "outer," depending on the position of the legs.

Common Movements.

1. Vaults, Mounts and Dismounts.
    a. Vaults—A vault is a jump over the apparatus with the hands supporting the body momentarily. It is done from floor to floor, from apparatus to floor or from floor to apparatus.
    b. Mounts—A mount is an interrupted vault ending in a position on the apparatus.
    c. Dismounts—Simply a vault or swing from the apparatus to the floor.
2. Front Vault. The gymnast faces the apparatus as she passes over.
3. Rear Vault. Gymnast's back is towards apparatus as she passes over.
4. Flank Vault. Gymnast's side is towards the apparatus as she passes over.
5. Squat, Straddle, Stoop or Wolf Vaults. These refer to the position of the legs as the body passes over the apparatus. See Figure 5-4.

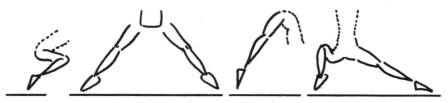

Figure 5-4.—Left to right, squat, straddle, stoop (pike) and wolf (squat-straddle)

6. Turns. A turn usually refers to a circular movement about the length axis. Occasionally, when the turn is very rapid, it is called a twist.
7. Circles. These movements are usually performed on a bar. To be a true circle the gymnast turns a full 360 degrees around the hands, knees or hips. When the circle is done with the front of the body facing the bar near the hips, it is a hip circle. If the rear of the body is next to the bar near the hips, any circle from this position is commonly called a seat circle. A circle can be done forward or backward depending whether the front or back of the gymnast leads.
8. Swings. Swings are simply incomplete circles with suspension from the hands or knees (hocks).
9. Casts. These are jerky swings in hang or support where most of the action is from the hips down. A kipping element is sometimes present.

55

10. Rolls. Usually a roll forward or backward over the curved spine.

11. Handsprings. A somersault forward or backward assisted by a spring from the hands.

12. Somersaults. A complete circle of the body in the air from feet to feet. Somersaults can be done forward, backward and sideward.

13. Kips (upstarts). This movement is especially descriptive of a snapping movement on a bar in which the body is lifted from a hang to a support. In most kips the body is first extended during the forward part of a swing then is quickly piked and extended again to arrive in support. These movements are also called swinging kips. "Dead" kips can be done on the floor or from a hang-lying position on the uneven bars. Since they are done without a preliminary swing they are often called "dead" kips.

14. Uprises (Stem rises, stems, swing stems). In German "stemmen" means a kind of propping lift. In this movement the arms act as a prop at the end of a forward or backward swing. There is first a pulling action followed by a pushing action and the body travels from a hang to support. On the uneven bars a stem rise commonly refers to a movement in which the body travels from a hang-stand on the low bar to a support on the high bar. Since the arms act as a prop, this movement truly qualifies as a stem movement.

15. Cuts. Leg movements from support where one leg swings under one of the supporting hands.

CONCLUSION

Perhaps there never will be a uniform nomenclature for gymnastics. As a gymnast, however, you will have a feeling of belonging once you start to speak like a gymnast. It is much like learning a foreign-language. It may be confusing to teachers but the gymnasts enjoy the creative side of their gymnastic language.

Some years ago, the writer and a group of girls invented the term, "Bardot" to describe a gymnastic backbend. The "Bardot" was the long, smooth, curving variety. We had formerly called it a "bridge." Since Brigitte Bardot was making news at the time for curves of her own, the term seemed especially nice to apply to this position.

The "Bardot" never did catch on in the gymnastic world but we nonetheless enjoyed the naming. It is this kind of creative fun that has held back an adoption of standard terminology. Why fight it?

All-Around Olympic Champion, Vera Caslavska, is shown in film drawings of her four Olympic optionals in Tokyo.

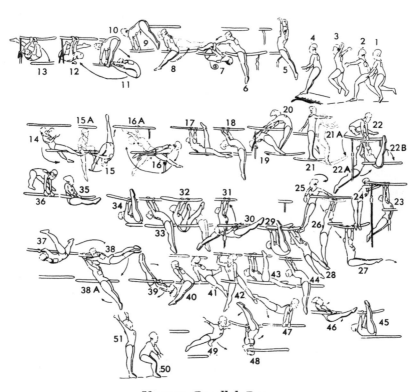

Uneven Parallel Bars

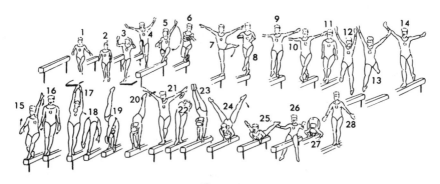

Beam

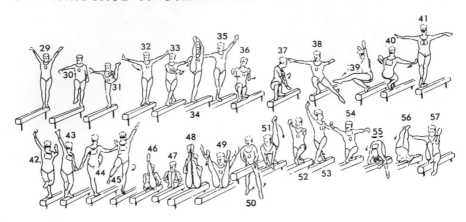

Beam

Beam

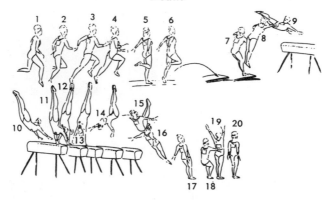

Vault

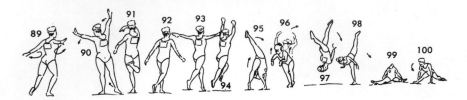

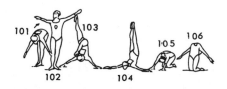

Floor Exercise

An Index to Advanced Gymnastic Skill

This chapter is devoted to a special index. The index contains a listing of the movements which were performed by the current Olympic and European All-Around Champion, Vera Caslavska. In her four optional routines in Tokyo, Caslavska covered the range of gymnastic movements very well. Her routine on the beam was rewarded with the gold medal for that event and were it not for one missed movement on the uneven bars, many experts believe she might have again won the gold medal. Her vault was good enough for a gold medal and her floor exercise was awarded sixth place even though she had a major fault. Her four compulsory exercises, the ones which were required of each Olympian and designed by the International Gymnastic Federation, were scored at 9.5 or better. A score of ten is perfect. Quite a record!

Movements appear in four categories, one for each of the events. The movements are placed in alphabetical order and each has a number which corresponds to the number appearing on the sequence drawings which are found on the front and back inside covers. Finally, many of the movements listed in the index have some added commentary to help explain them. As you look at the drawings remember that Caslavska is moving rapidly in most instances. Try to see how one of her movements leads into the next movement. *Note: The four prints appearing in this chapter were especially prepared by Ivan Foster, an outstanding Delaware artist and friend of the author.*

INDEX TO A CHAMPION GYMNAST

Floor Exercise (F)

Action-Reaction—These movements are listed especially to show how a movement in one direction aids the action of a movement in another direction.
F(3-4); F(16-18); F(41-42); F(56-58) and F(74-75). How many others
can you pick out?

Aerial Cartwheel—F(35-38) In this sequence you will see how the moving
splits action helps the gymnast. Her tremendous kick F(35-36) actually
lifts her off the ground. Since her splits are good, she can maintain her
standing height on the L. leg a bit longer. Once in the air, the same leg
moves rapidly for a landing.

Aerial Roundoff—F(38-41)

Arabesque (momentary)—F-14 To perform this very effective movement, she
lunges her body quickly into the arabesque and follows immediately with
a run. (F-15)

Backbending—F(31-32) There is backbending and backbending. This variety is particularly difficult due to the balancing aspect.

Backbending—F(102-104) From a stand F-102, the gymnast bends back to her hands passing through a wide arm handstand (F-103) finally chest rolling out to F-104.

Back Handspring—F(41-45) This movement is slowed down a bit as shown in F-44 in order that a soft landing on the knees will result. In F-44 the gymnast purposely lets some of her weight go forward in order to produce this soft landing. Ordinarily this would not be good form for this movement since any continuous backward movement resulting from the landing would have to be terrifically forced if done at all. The back handspring landing which enables the gymnast to coordinate it with other movements is similar to the figures in F-19 and F-96 where Caslavska is finishing a roundoff.

Back Somersault (full twisting)—F(20-26) This is one of Caslavska's poorest movements and may have resulted in the largest deduction that she received for any of her movements presented in this book. Her height is very low as her twist is completed in F-24 and you will note an apparent collapse in F-25-26). Being the great gymnast that she is, she recoups rapidly and turns rearward immediately into splits. (27-30)

Cartwheel (left)—F(85-88) The starting position F-85 is not the standard one since she has just completed an "illusion." Once again, as seen in F-87, she takes advantage of the splits stretch and thus performs a better looking cartwheel.

Chest Roll—F-104

Handspring (forward to straddle seat)—F(59-63) A good skip step precedes the action which is slowed down somewhat since the landing on the feet will not be as in the regular forward handspring. Notice the straight leg kick (F-60) which is good form for all handsprings. The movement is completed by straddling the legs in mid-air (F-61) and the shock of landing is first taken by the feet in wide base (F-62) before actually coming to the seat in F-63.

Illusion—F(82-85) In this movement the weight remains on one stretched leg while the body rotates around as shown. It is like doing a cartwheel while standing and pivoting on one foot. An illusion requires good splits flexibility.

Kick (high kick)—F-1

Knee Balance—F-106 From a low stand, the gymnast arches her back to a balance.

Kneeling (a low kneeling pose)—F-46

Leap—F(10-12) A leap can be broadly defined as a forward jump taking off from one foot and landing on the opposite foot. Caslavska plants her R. foot (F-10) and lands on her L. foot (F-12).

Leap (legs split)—F(56-58) Since this leap is higher than her previous leaps (F-10 to F-12 and F-53 to F-56), she accelerates the lead leg by bending it at the knee, thus getting it into the air faster (F-57). She gets into a perfect splits position (F-58) before landing.

Roundoff (to convert forward speed into backward action—F(15-19) The action is similar (though faster) to a cartwheel with a ¼ turn.

Roundoff—F(94-96) Notice how this roundoff and the one shown in F(15-19) is preceded by a good run and skip step.

Skip Step (R. foot hop, immediate turn R.) F(6-8) A skip step is used to accelerate the action of movements which follow it. From a run, the gymnast simply hops on either the R. or L. foot. This is followed immediately by a step. Usually the gymnast will be one-sided, almost always hopping on the same foot. Caslavska uses skip steps with the hops taking place on both the L. and the R. feet. She favors a R. hop however, indicating she may be right-handed in a majority of her movements.

Skip Step (R. foot hop)—F(16-17) Notice the good stretch of the gymnast in F-16 prior to the landing on the R. foot. This stretch, seen in all of Caslavska's skip steps, assures her of the greatest possible momentum for the movement to follow.

Skip Step (R. foot hop)—F-34

Skip Step (L. foot hop)—F-59

Skip Step (R. foot hop)—F(91-94) The gymnast starts from a unique stance (you name it) which we have also seen Caslavska do on the beam (B-63). She runs, shows excellent stretch on her hop once again (F-94) and proceeds to do a roundoff.

Somersault (back layout to one foot)—F(96-98) Here again a good skip step, round off and arm throw (F-96 dotted) enable the gymnast to achieve the needed height. To further insure a good movement she splits the legs prior to landing (F-98). She is flexible enough to quickly thrust the leg down to a stand.

Splits or Splits Position—F-1, F-18, F-30, F-37, F-39, F-58, F-65, F-83, F-87, F-98 and F-99.

Splits—F(29-30) Although the gymnast is moving fairly rapidly in this sequence, a slow variety of the same movement is recommended as an exercise leading to the development of splits. This is the forward-backward splits as opposed to the side splits where the legs are widely straddled.

Splits (rear turn to splits)—F(63-65) The movement preceding the action in this sequence is sometimes called a rear turn mount especially when performed on apparatus. Caslavska has developed momentum from the handspring so she simply rides forward (F-63) while turning to her L. and swinging the L. leg in a wide arc (F-64) until she comes to splits (F-65).

Splits—F(98-99) The gymnast has just completed a back somersault to one foot. Note the L. leg is already in splits position. She merely falls rearward to complete the movement. (F-99)

Standing Up—F(46-49) How many ways can you stand up . . . gymnastically? This sequence shows one of thousands of ways you might try. What other movements might have been selected by Caslavska to get out of her kneeling position? (F-46)

Stand-up (from splits)—F(65-68) The gymnast swings her front leg (now bent) under the back leg in order to kneel on it. She then steps forward with the L. leg and stands.

Stretched Stand (L. foot)—F-2 This position is very similar to the stance taken to start a cartwheel.

Stretched Stand (on toes; feet together)—F-5 Notice the flexibility of the back.

Stretched Stand—F-13 Stand done on L. foot with opposite knee bent close to chest. Remember that many of these stretched stands are very momentary. The film drawings were made at the point of greatest stretch in each case.

Stretched Stand (momentary arabesque)—F-33

Stretched Stand—F-49 Note that the toe of the foot in the rear barely touches the floor.

Turn (¾ L.)—F(2-5) From a stretched stand on the L. foot in F-2, the gymnast steps R. (F-3) crossing her arms in front of her body. As the turn continues to F-4, the arms "fling" to a new position. In F-5 the R. foot is drawn forward and she stretches once again.

Turn (a running turn)—F(8-10) This kind of turn is seen frequently in girls' floor exercise. The movement rounds off what might otherwise be a very sharp corner in the floor movement pattern. Smooth, curving patterns are preferred to the more masculine sharp ones.

Turn (rearways)—F(27-28) This is a turn rearways to the gymnast's L. followed by a step into splits.

Turn (full turn R.)—F(68-72) The "cocking" action L. in F-68 provides the turning momentum. She pivots on her L. foot (F-69); steps R. (F-70); then pivots on her R. foot to a stretched (momentary) stand on her R. foot (F-72).

Turn (full turn R.)—F(73-79) This turn is basically the same as the one shown from F-68 to F-72 but in this turn the L. leg makes a wider sweep (F-77).

If you have followed Caslavska's movements carefully you have seen that she stretches whenever she can not only to make her exercise more beautiful but to take full advantage of the body's levering qualities which are explained in Chapter 4. Her ability to split helps her to achieve superior difficulty. On the other hand, many of her movements can be performed by the novice. What a pity that you cannot see the movements and hear the music combined, for it is to this totality we refer when we speak of the floor exercise event! An approximation of Caslavska's floor pattern is found in Figure 6-1.

Caslavska's winning vault in Tokyo was a piked handspring known as a Yamashita. The name has come into popular use to honor Haruhiro Yamashita who has been credited with the early competitive use of the vault.

Action-Reaction—V(7-8) and V(11-13)

Jump to the Board (two foot landing)—V(5-7) The gymnast recovers her R. knee rapidly in V(5-6) joining the legs as the jump is in progress. The landing (V-7) shows the feet joined with the gymnast just touching the board. Her body is properly flexed as she prepares to coordinate her body for the preflight (on flight) jump.

Landing—V(17-20) The gymnast's landing is ideal. She bends slightly at the knees upon arriving on the mat. Her body is just back of a vertical position.

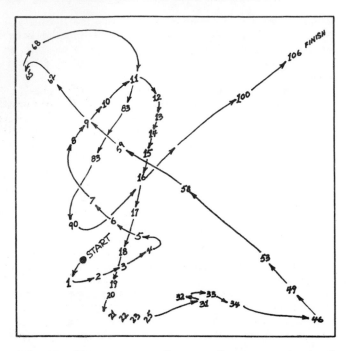

Figure 6-1.—Numbers correspond to numbers in sequence drawings

She quickly stretches to a stand with her arms held in "dislocate" position. Photographs taken of Caslavska at the moment of landing show a victorious smile. She seemed to say, "All of the months of training and hard work made possible this split second of joy." She "stuck" her landing. This means that her feet did not move after she touched down and she had control of her body. She won the gold medal and received for this vault a score which averaged nearly 9.8. She really "hit" her vault, meaning she performed it very well.

Layout—V(7-10) The layout portion of the vault has come to mean that portion of the vault just preceding the push-off. All advanced vaults with a rating of 10 are often called the layout series. Caslavska's vault should rightfully be called a layout piked handspring. Notice that in V-8 the gymnast takes off with a definite vertical direction, though somewhat angled towards the horse. This upward direction is characteristic of all good vaults. A vaulter does not dive directly to the horse. She shows excellent preflight (on flight) in V-9 even though at this time she may have as much as a foot more to travel before contacting the horse with her hands. In V-10 her body has rotated forward and her hands are about to touch. At the actual point of touch, she will be in an excellent position (due to her height) to push off and complete her vault. As height in preflight decreases the push off becomes increasingly more difficult and there is a tendency

Evaluation Questions

Action-reaction movements are included in each of the four sections of the Index. By which of Newton's three laws are such movements governed?

to slow down. Such is not the case with Caslavska. Because of the excellent position she shows in V-10 she will be able to maintain her speed and actually get additional height from her push off.

Off Flight—V(14-17) The gymnast at position V-14 has passed the critical points of the vault with flying colors. A good run, jump, height and push

Side Horse Vault (V)

off have preceded this position and the final 'hurdle," the landing, is all that remains. The high, piked position in V-15 is beautiful. In V-16 the gymnast looks for her landing but she is otherwise well stretched. Achieving a stretch in this downward flight is an important component of vaulting. If Caslavska had any imperfection at all it was probably at V-16.

Push Off—V(11-13) Here we observe the pushing efforts of the gymnast. This occurs both with the hands and by a definite stretch through the shoulders. Notice that in V-13 the push is almost vertical.

Running—V(1-4) Running is the key to a good vault. Note in particular the gymnast's posture in V-3. Caslavska has good running form measured by the track and field standard. Without correct running form advanced layout vaults are usually very poorly done.

Action-Reaction—B(6-7), B(40-41), B(49-51) and B(58-59)

Balance (sitting in tight pike)—B(46-48) In B-46 the gymnast prepares for this difficult balance hold. Slowly the legs are tucked in B-47. She then very slowly stretches her legs until they are very close to her head. Notice

Balance Beam (B)

that her hands are not on the beam, thus making the balance more difficult. She held position B-48 long enough to show control and mastery
of the balance.

Balance—B(42-43) The gymnast steps backward with the R. foot (B-42)
placing the top of her R. foot on the beam while bending the L. leg
slightly. The arms, held diagonally, make a straight line and balance out
the position of the legs.

Balance (pose)—B(51-53) From a knee scale, the gymnast swings the back
leg down to place the foot diagonally on the beam in front of the body.
She stands slowly slightly turning R. and with a quick hand movement she
shows the momentary pose position in B-53.

Balance (asymmetrical pose)—B-63 The gymnast steps L. in B-62 and immediately
swings into the pose in B-63. Note that the R. leg and the L. arm are
bent while the R. arm and the L. leg are stretched. This asymmetrical pose
is held only momentarily and provides a delightful break in a simple walk.

Balance (one leg in squat; one leg stretched forward)—B5 This is similar to
the print showing a gymnast on the beam.

Balance (momentary front scale; arms side upward)—B(6-7) In B-6 the gymnast coils by crossing her arms. As she flings the arms sideward and
upward this motion of the arms helps her to stand gracefully. Although
she is moving in this sequence, she might have held the position. There
may be as many as three held positions on the beam after which the
gymnast is penalized. Note the high position of the rear leg. Even with
the trunk held vertically, it is parallel with the beam.

Back Roll (head on the beam)—B(26-28) This movement is often confused
with a back shoulder roll which is less difficult. In the latter the head comes
off the beam and as a rule it is done more slowly. The back roll permits
a higher position of the hips, enabling the gymnast to stand with relative
ease (B-28). This is not possible in the typical shoulder roll.

Back Walkover—B(16-21) The arm circles seen in B(15-16) lead the movement
thus making it smooth. In B-18 you will see that the gymnast is now
supported by only a single foot and she is falling. Some girls have very
loose backs and are able to do this movement with absolute balance until
the hands make contact. This latter movement is less difficult and more
acrobatic in nature. The element of danger is obvious in the Caslavska
sequence. Without this element of danger, the movement cannot be
classified as a real difficulty.

Cartwheel—B(68-70) Notice particularly the splits position of the legs going
into and coming out of the cartwheel. Better control of balance results
since in bending the legs other levers develop thus complicating the
balance control.

Cast (to a knee scale)—B (49-51) As the legs are straddled (to B-49), the
gymnast quickly reaches through her legs to grasp the beam. Between B-50
and B-51 she holds her weight momentarily on her hands allowing a gentle
descent of the knee to the beam.

Forward Roll—B(54-57) Starting from the R. knee with the L. leg straight and
about to slide down the side of the beam (B-54), she places her hands
along the sides of the beam and rolls forward. The head is in contact with
the beam in B-55 and B-56. The direction of the roll is felt on the spine

and any action to either side is controlled with the hands. She finishes by placing her R. foot on the beam while the L. leg swings down (B-57) and provides the swing-momentum needed for the stand which follows.

Handstand (straddle down—a form of chest roll)—B(23-26) Notice the bend of the arms as the legs are lowered. This makes for a gentle and controlled roll down.

High Kick (legs in splits position during the kick of R. leg)—B(33-35) The preparatory movement is seen in B-33 as the gymnast swings both arms to her left then raises them thus leading the kick of the R. leg.

Jump (mount)—B(1-4) Without the use of her hands and with a single foot take-off, the gymnast uses the board and powerful arm lift to arrive on the beam with a single foot.

Jump (leap)—B(10-14) This movement is a simple leap from the L. foot to the R. foot. Notice how the gymnast swings her arms down (B-11) as the body bends slightly in preparation for the leap.

Knee Scale—B-51 Notice the high, curved stretch of the L. leg.

Lunge—B(64-65) The gymnast steps R. (B-64) in a lunge (B-65) with the R. arm stretched upward.

Lunge—B(35-36) In preparing to lunge, the gymnast gives a stylish little tap to the shin of the supporting leg (B-35) and then lunges it forward to B-36.

Scale (momentary; step into)—B(29-31) Notice how this scale, again momentary, is different than the one in B-7. Actually these momentary positions might simply be called stretched stands on a single foot. A true scale is usually a held position.

Somersault (layout; dismount)—B(70-75) Immediately upon the completion of the preceding cartwheel, the gymnast throws up and back stretching the legs B-72) to a layout back somersault (B-73). She looks for her landing in B-73 and B-74. In B-75 her landing is completed. Her legs bend no farther than shown in B-75 and being slightly off balance she steps quickly to B-76. Finally she stands in B-77. Except for the slight step, Caslavska showed excellent control of her landing in this very difficult dismount. The writer more often than not has seen such a dismount (very seldom laid out) overthrown so that the gymnast invariably falls backward to her hips. This is a serious error which might be penalized by a full point deduction.

Splits Position of Legs—B-19, B-34, B-70 and B-69

Stand—B-57, B-58 Using her swinging L. leg and a downward-backward-upward swing of the arms, the gymnast stands on her R. foot and places the L. foot diagonally forward on the beam in front of her R. foot (B-58). Notice once again in B-58 that the R. foot is curled under and both knees show a slight bend.

Stretched Stand—B(40-41) This movement gains momentum from the arms. In B-40 the gymnast is about to cross her arms in front of her body which is in squat stand. The arms are immediately uncrossed and raised sidewards, thus assisting the body to stand with ease. In standing, her L. foot is brought to the rear of her R. foot. (A backward step) Caslavska uses the arm crossing and uncrossing many times on beam and floor to provide momentum. Have you noticed?

Stretch to Stand—B(58-59) From the bent position in B-58, with arms crossed in front of her body, the arms swing outward and upward as the gymnast rises high on the L. foot.

Steps—B(8-10), B(14-15), B(29-30), B(32-33), B(41-43), B(58-62) and B(67-68) Notice in these sequences that there is a definite turn out of the feet. The feet are placed diagonally on the beam rather than parallel with it. At times you may actually see the toes gripping the side of the beam. This position provides a greater support and a more confident feel for the gymnast, although it is not usually a natural movement for the beginner.

Step and Pivot Turn at End of Beam—B(57-62) The gymnast steps R. (B-57) and while pivoting on her R. foot her L. leg is swung in a small arc around the end of the beam (B-60 to B-61). In B-62 her L. leg continues to swing forward and is placed on the beam in front of the R. foot.

Turn (½ single leg squat turn)—B(37-40) The movement starts with a "cocking" action of the arms in B-37. The arms are swung around to the R. They are followed shortly by the back leg which has been stretched in the lunge preceding the movement. The impetus thus provides a rotating action around the support foot of the gymnast and she completes a half circle to her R. During the course of her exercise, Caslavska turns only five times. Each of these turns was 180 degrees or a half turn. Other turns are found in B(38-40), B(45-46), B(60-61) and B(65-66).

Uneven Parallel Bars (U)

Action-Reaction—The gymnast's "cocking" action is evident in the following sequences . . . U-8, U(4-5), U-15, U(17-19), U-21, U(22-23), U(33-34) and U(47-50).

Cast—U-8 In preparation for the cast, the gymnast swings her legs under the bar and then casts to the dotted position.

Cast (to stoop or pike stand on low bar) U(8-11) Notice how the head and shoulders of Caslavska are forward of the bar in U-9. This action maintains the center of weight over the bar for balance to allow time for the feet to be placed properly as shown in U-10.

Cast (to straddle position of the legs)—U(35-36) The cast here is done to a straddle position rather than a stand on the bar. Her weight is held slightly behind the bar and she is well stretched for the straddle swing which follows.

Cast (and single leg cut)—U(40-43) The cut (U-41) is followed by a half turn to a hang-lying position with the R. leg held vertical to the low bar. U-17 shows the same position with the L. leg up.

Cast—U-47 In this cast Caslavska prepares herself for the hip circle which follows.

Circle (½ single leg circle to hang lying position on low bar)—U(16-17) From U-16 (dotted) her L. leg swings around and up to the position shown in U-17.

Circle (hip circle backwards)—U(38-40) This movement is commonly called a wrap-around. Intermediate gymnasts learn the wrap-around from a long hang facing the low bar so that the swing is from under the low bar. In this sequence Caslavska performs a more difficult variety from the other side.

Circle (hip circle forward)—U(5-8) Here you will observe a wonderful example of bar circling since both important aspects of all circles are dramatically shown. First it is important to stretch out prior to the downward portion of the circle. You see such a stretch in U-5. In the portion of the circle where the gymnast is rising, it is important to pull in towards the bar. Caslavska achieves this quality by tucking (U-7). Her momentum was so great in this sequence that she actually travelled around the low bar twice and had speed to spare for the cast shown in U-8.

Circle (feint wrap-around)—U(22A-22B) In U(22A-22B) Caslavska shows the normal approach for the wrap-around on the low bar. She might have released the high bar in U-22B to complete a hip circle backward but she used this action to "cock" her body for another kind of movement. Following U-22B she cast backward to an uprise (stem rise). The word "feint" is often used in gymnastics to describe a "cocking" movement in one direction which supplies swing for a movement in the opposite direction.

Circle (½ single knee circle forward)—U-15 Having hooked her knee on the bar in U-14, the gymnast drops backward to a hang (notice the splits position of the legs) and, hooking her knee once again, returns to U-15 (dotted).

Circle (½ stoop circle backwards)—U(9-11) In U-11 you will again notice the tremendous effort to stretch the body as the gymnast travels down with gravity. She needs all the momentum she can muster since she will let go shortly after passing under the low bar to catch the high bar (U-12).

Circle (½ straddle circle, ½ turn to long hang over low bar)—U(36-38) From U-37 to U-38 the gymnast shows a variety of kipping action with a ½ turn. This same action is often described as an under bar cast with or without the ½ turn.

Circle (¾ Mill circle forward)—U-16 This movement is sometimes called a crotch circle but most girls prefer "Mill circle." The stretch on the downward portion of the circle is again apparent.

Crotch Circle—U-16

Front Support—U-8, U-40 and U-47 Although the gymnast is moving in all of the references, they qualify as front supports (momentary) although none are of the "rest" variety. In U-47 the support is called a "free" support.

Glide—U(27-28) This movement is one of preparation for a variety of kipping actions. One of the easiest is a single knee uprise. Caslavska chooses one of the more difficult kips following her glide. She kips, releasing the low bar to a catch on the high bar.

Hang-Stand—U-19

Hang (long hang)—U(22A and 23) The term "long hang" is very commonly used to describe hangs from the high bar. The term is very rarely used by boys and men.

Hang-Lying Position (body arched)—U-18 Practice moving from U-17 to U-18. You should feel a nice stretching or "cocking" action which will enable you to do a number of movements following the stretch. A hang-lying position (rearways) is also shown in U-33.

Hecht ("Bird") *Dismount*—U(47-50) This dismount is normally performed out of a wrap-around (hip circle backward). The gymnast lets go early, shortly after U-48 and literally bounces away from the bar. Caslavska chose to do her Hecht on the high bar and travel over the low bar which is much more dangerous than the similar dismount on the low bar. She had previously used this dismount in an international competition and had a serious fall when her foot hooked the low bar as she passed over it. (See U-49) Although the Hecht is now a popular dismount for girls it was once almost exclusively attributed to Mrs. Doris Fuchs Brause, one of the finest gymnasts in the United States. It is some wonder that it is not called a "Fuchs" today. The word "Hecht" comes to us from the German language and means "atop" or "going over." Since birds are often "atop" or "going over" something, the term "Bird" is often applied to the movement. "Bird" is especially used for "Hecht" when the legs are straddled as shown by Caslavska in U-49.

Hip Circle Backward—U(47-48)

Jump (dismount landing)—U(50-51) From a slightly bent knee position, the gymnast stretches (arms in "dislocate" position) to a stand.

Jump (arched)—U-5

Kip (from hang-lying rearways on low bar to support on high bar)—U(33-35) and U(44-46) The gymnast has completed her arching action (typical for a kip) in U-33. She immediately whips the feet to the high bar (U-34) then extends her legs along the high bar rapidly to arrive at U-35.

Kip (glide kip)—U(27-30) Of particular interest in this sequence is the straddled position of the legs during the glide portion of the movement (U-28). This action helps to decrease the lever length of the legs making it less likely that the feet will touch when the body is fully extended. Caslavska dropped into her glide with great speed and she needed exceptionally good abdominal strength to keep her feet from touching; hence the leg straddle in U-28.

Long Hang—U-22A and U-23

Long Hang (from a long hang, straddle the low bar to a hang-lying position)— U(31-32)

Mill Circle (¾ circle)—U-16

Release and Catch—U(11-12) The release and catch work on the uneven bars separate the intermediate performer from the advanced performer. No movement is considered a real difficulty without this kind of action. In this sequence, Caslavska performs half a stoop circle, release and catches the high bar in a pike-straddle hang.

Release and Catch—U(12-14) From an inverted pike-straddle hang, the gymnast turns to her R. dropping to a single knee hang on the low bar.

Release and Catch—U-16 From a ¾ Mill circle, the gymnast releases the low bar and catches the high bar. This movement is commonly seen in intermediate work.

Release and Catch—U(24-26) This is an extremely difficult movement. During this very movement in Tokyo, Caslavska on her first attempt failed to regrasp the high bar and dropped to the floor for which she received a full point deduction. Even so, she was able to finish in the first ten in this event due to her excellent performance in the compulsory phase of the uneven bar competition and because the exercise described in this book was of such high caliber, even though she had an unfortunate "break." This movement would be described as a rear uprise, release, with a full turn to a regrasp on the high bar.

Release and Catch—U(26-27) In this sequence (following her second attempt at the full turn and catch which was successful) she quickly grips the high bar (U-26) to establish a forward direction for her body. She releases immediately and drops to regrasp the low bar.

Release and Catch—U(29-31) From a glide kip on the low bar, the gymnast releases the low bar and regrasps the high bar.

Running—U(1-4) As seen in the film, Caslavska had an unusually long run in order to hit the board and acquire the proper height for her mount.

Splits (position of the legs)—U-15 and U-16 U-15 (solid line) shows the tremendous stretch effort of the gymnast to get her body away from the bar at the critical time. (See circles)

Stand (arched on low bar)—U-20

Straddle-Catch Backwards—U-(21-22)

Supple Movement (a kind of body wave)—U(19-20) From a stand-hang, the gymnast forces her body through her arms and under the high bar to arrive at a stand on the low bar. She releases neither her feet or hands during the movement.

Uprise (rear uprise, stem rise)—U(22B-24) Using the tremendous casting power of the feint wrap-around (U-22B), the gymnast casts backward through a long hang continuing upward until her shoulders are above the high bar (U-25).

Wrap-Around (See hip circle backward)—U(22A-22B)

7

The Code of Points . . . . The Gymnast's Rule Book

If you decide that you would like to enter gymnastic competition, you must become familiar with The Code of Points[5] for women. The Code is issued by the International Gymnastic Federation and is published in the French language. Governing federations in each country then translate the Code and publish it in their native languages.

The Code is really an international standard for gymnastic performance. It is important for a competitor to know how she rates gymnastically in the eyes of the world.

In most countries the local gymnastic federations have established national standards of performance to protect budding gymnasts from entering advanced competition before they have a chance to develop in the fundamentals. These federations have prepared exercises for each of the contested events. Such exercises are called compulsory exercises. Sets of exercises can be prepared for as many as nine levels of competition.

The gymnasts entering the lower levels of competition are required to perform these prescribed exercises. An exercise is prescribed for floor exercise, beam and uneven bars and a vault is selected.

At the upper levels, each gymnast will do two exercises (or vaults) for each event. One of these is prescribed by the federation; the other is an exercise or vault of the gymnast's choice. The latter is known as an optional exercise. It is the feeling of these federations that only gymnasts at the upper levels of competition should attempt to compose their routines

---

[5]English translation of The Code of Points can be obtained from The Amateur Athletic Union of the United States. 231 W. 58th St., New York, N.Y. ($1.25)

since they have the background and motivation to do so. We have not quite arrived at this philosophy in the United States but we are slowly progressing in this direction.

The United States Gymnastic Federation has released a Workbook[6] which outlines a set of graded exercises. These exercises have been adopted for use in girls' competition in school systems throughout the United States. Some groups have eliminated optional exercises in meets where beginners or intermediates compete. The United States is one of few countries where organized competition for children of elementary school age flourishes. This presents a problem when the very young are not prepared properly in fundamentals and then are asked to do optional exercises. When only prescribed exercises are used for this latter group, there are fewer problems.

Judging gymnastics is one of the most difficult officiating jobs in the entire world of sport. Judges may be called upon to evaluate both compulsory and optional exercises.

Judging compulsory exercises is less difficult than judging optional work. The judge knows what the performer will attempt to do. Her evaluation of the exercise will be in terms of how well the gymnast has complied with the requirements of that exercise. She will have an opportunity to study these requirements long before she is called upon to judge.

None of the foregoing is true about judging the optional exercise, however. The optional judge does *not* know exactly what the performer will do. She must rate the optional exercise by applying the Code of Points.

The judge may award a maximum of ten points for a perfect exercise. Generally speaking, a gymnast gets up to five points for *what* she does and up to five points for *how* she does her exercise. In short, there are "What" points and "How" points.

Three of the "What" points are awarded for difficulty. The gymnast must have five elements of difficulty, one of which must be exceptionally difficult. Difficulty value will often be a matter of opinion since the women, unlike the men, do not define and grade difficult movements per se, although the International Federation does publish a general list of difficulties.

Two of the "What" points are awarded for the composition of the exercise. In this portion of the score, the judge attempts to evaluate the

---

[6]*Age Group Workbook* obtained from the United States Gymnastic Federation, P.O. Box 4699, Tucson, Arizona. ($2.00)

technical value of the exercise. In short, does it fit all of the requirements outlined in the Code for composition? These requirements are discussed briefly below under each of the four events.

The "How" points are not as clearly defined as the "What" points. This aspect of judging becomes more or less an artistic appraisal. A section of the "How" points is devoted to what is known as "General Impression." This is the most elusive section of the Code. The judge will consider general appearance and bearing. She looks for elegance, grace and ease of performance. Attire must also be satisfactory. Underclothes, for example, should match the color of the leotard. The important, more tangible area of the "How" points is the judging of the execution of an exercise. The table in Figure 7-1 gives you a general idea of the scope of deductions for faults in an optional exercise. Unlike the compulsory, which lists a specific deduction for each malexecuted component, the schedule shown

SCHEDULE OF DEDUCTIONS (F.I.G.)*

Reason For Deduction	Minor Deductions .1-.2	Median Deductions .3-.5	Major Deductions .6+
Unnecessary Bending or adjustment	Toe point; hand faults; head non-alined; slight knee bend or arm bend; slight body bend or leg straddle (45°)	Medium bend in arms, legs, body or leg straddles 45°-90°) V—Pre-flight bend	Extreme bending V—Body bend before inverted support (M 1.00) V—Bending arms in support (M 1.00) V—Arms completely bent 2.50
Movements showing lack of extension or height	Slight lack of height	Median lack of height	Complete lack of height V—Preflight (M 1.50)
Balance faults	Slight imbalance on dismounts but with no foot movement .10 (same fault with step or hop .2) V—Heavy landing .2 B—Arm or leg movements to maintain balance	Obvious shifts of trunk or arms (sans pieds) to maintain balance Fall after dismount with support of one or both hands B—Touching with hands for balance .5 B—Support of hands for balance 1.00	Arm support on dismount Landing with a fall Hit floor with pelvis or knees Unjustified support in any movement V—V—Knees touch 1.50 V—Hips touch 2.00 V—Hand support (landing) 1.0
Unjustified stops or pauses	Slight rhythmic pause UPB—Each stop .2 B—Monotonous rhythm	Stopping, between parts Lack of continuity V—Stopping, in handstand	General uneven or "jerky" performance
Touching floor or apparatus involuntarily	Slight (to level position)	With support of fingertips V—Touch horse with feet	Extensive support with hands
Support faults	Support with delay of an arm	Pronounced unevenness in support	Supplemental support V—Gaining support with strength (M 1.00)
Hand repulsion & leap extension faults	Minor difficulty	Extension incomplete Late repulsion of hands	No extension Delayed hand push V—Failure to straighten body after flight 2.00 V—Lacks push-off (M 1.00)
Other faults	Poor bearing F.X. Steps out (.10 each time)	Coach speaks to performer F.X. Coach in area	Coach assists performer Music incorrect (M 1.00) Reversal of part of ex.

F.X.—Floor Exercise   B.—Balance Beam   V.—Vaulting   UPB.—Uneven Parallel Bars

Help during vault = Zero (Assist on landing—2.00)

*By permission of *The Modern Gymnast Magazine.*

Figure 7-1

in Figure 7-1 must be applied to an exercise that is usually unknown to the judge.

FLOOR EXERCISE "WHATS"

In the floor exercise event, you have from one minute to one minute and a half to show your competency. Your space or "floor" is an area 39′ x 39′. You must cover this area thoroughly and show that you have mastered the fundamentals by executing the following kinds of body movement and skill:

1. Movements through a momentary handstand
2. Turns, rolls and jumps
3. Balances (If a position is held, you should show control.)
4. Demonstration of back flexibility
5. Splits
6. Sequences from dance and ballet
7. Connecting movements and change of pace

Your composition will be made up of many movements and non-movements which must be closely synchronized with music. A single instrument such as a piano, flute or drum is used to provide your musical needs. This is the really difficult part of the floor exercise—the harmony of gymnastic movement to music. A useful technique for choreographing a gymnastic free exercise has been described by the author.[7]

You will plan your exercise so that various suitable elements are sprinkled throughout the exercise. Planning an exercise takes a great deal of knowledge and experience. The help of a coach is essential.

VAULTING "WHATS"

Your vault will be judged much as if it were a fancy dive. Each vault has a maximum value assigned. These values usually range from 7.5 to 10.0. This maximum value is awarded only if the vault is perfectly executed. The major difference between vaulting and diving is that in vaulting you need not announce your vault in advance. You get credit for what you do even if it is somewhat different from the vault you thought you would do. You are required to do two optional vaults. They may be two different vaults.

In vaulting, you propel your body over the horse using the hands for momentary support. The chart in Figure 7-1 outlines the major faults of vaulting and the associated penalties. Basically you are judged on what

---

[7]Frederick, A. B. "Draw Your Free Exercise Music," *Madamoiselle Gymnast,* April, 1966. (Vol. I, No. 2)

you do before you touch the horse with your hands and what you do after the hands have touched (on flight and off flight). Both aspects of flight must show good distance for a superior score. Your landing will be watched carefully. It should be a controlled landing. If it is otherwise, points are deducted commensurate with the degree of the fault.

BALANCE BEAM "WHATS"

Your composition on the beam is really a floor exercise done on the very limited surface provided. The beam is approximately four inches wide and sixteen feet long. With such a restriction, balancing is naturally the major task no matter what skill or movement is attempted. The emphasis is placed on naturalness of performance. When the judge can forget that you are on a beam, you will have entered the advanced level, everything else being equal.

The exercise should be dynamic with variations in rhythm so it is not monotonous. You must stay on the beam for 80 seconds and no longer than 105 seconds. You must exhibit turning ability and show that you can leap from the beam and return with control. Other movement requirements conform to those for floor exercise. It is very likely that in the future exercises on the balance beam will also be done in harmony with music. At any rate it is a good practice to work with music while on the beam since it promotes free flowing work.

UNEVEN PARALLEL BAR "WHATS"

Swinging exercise rather than supported exercise is the basic difference between parallel bar work for men and women. Supports are only momentary and balances or holds should be especially appropriate for the bars. When you reach the point where you can do many movements in which you let go of a bar and then regrasp, you will have entered the advanced or difficult stage denoted by the Code.

Your exercise on the bars should not be punctuated with obvious stops or wasted movements. Continuous, meaningful movement is the rule as it is for floor exercise and beam work.

CONCLUSION

To be a competitor you must seek the guidance of a trained coach in gymnastics. She'll get you over the rough spots. Your progress will ultimately depend on cooperative efforts by you and your coach. It is a most rewarding experience and one which will be remembered for a lifetime. The Code of Points is your silent coach.

To be successful as a competitive gymnast get to know them both.

Where to Get Help
For Gymnastics

People, organizations, publications, periodicals and books are sources of help for the gymnast whether she be novice or advanced.

The physical educator at your school will be a prime source of help. You might ask her to let you know about participation clinics which are occasionally open to students and teachers alike. If you are fortunate enough to have a gymnastic club in your town you should seek out the instructors there. You will often find that the club instructors will have a great knowledge of gymnastics since many of them have devoted a lifetime to this specialty.

The following organizations will be helpful in locating the nearest affiliate of their national body.

1. The American Turners—1550 Clinton Ave. N., Rochester 21, N.Y.
2. American Sokol—5611 Cermak Rd., Cicero 50, Illinois.

These two organizations have celebrated their centennials in recent years and both have been devoted to a preservation of the cutural heritage of the countries from which their members originally emigrated. The Turners were exclusively from Germany while the Sokol organizations represent Slovak nations. Both organizations have been instrumental in fostering gymnastic programs and many national gymnastic champions have come from their ranks.

The Divison for Girls and Women's Sports of the American Association for Health, Physical Education and Recreational provides a unique service. The Division maintains a list of gymnastic leaders who are found in each of the fifty states and you may request a list of names of those leaders who are closest to your town. (DGWS—AAHPER—1201 16th St., N.W., Washington 36, D.C.)

Another source of help is the publication known as *The Modern Gymnast*. This periodical is the only one published in the United States which specializes in the sport of gymnastics and it is known around the world. If you have special problems you may request information from the staff of consultants associated with the magazine. You may get a reply by mail or read the reply in the "Letters" column. Due to the increased interest in gymnastics for girls, *The Modern Gymnast* staff has recently begun the publication of a quarterly entitled *Madamoiselle Gymnast*. (*The Modern Gymnast*—P.O. Box 611, Santa Monica, California.)

Some of the better books for gymnastics are listed below. These are in addition to those which have already been mentioned in footnotes.

Allison, June, *Advanced Gymnastics for Women*. London: Stanley Paul and Co. Ltd., 1963. Presents an excellent organization of gymnastic movements for all Olympic apparatus for women. Very readable. Illustrated.

Cooper, Phyllis, *Feminine Gymnastics*. Minneapolis: Burgess Publishing Co. Illustrated with film drawing sequences.

Drury, Blanche and Andrea Molnar, *Gymnastics for Women*. Palo Alto, Cal.: The National Press, 1964. Covers basic movement, ballet, ball work and other hand apparatus as well as listing gymnastic movements.

Frederick, A. B., *Gymnastic Action Cards*. Minneapolis: Burgess Publishing Co., 1965. Ninety-seven cards, each with a typical gymnastic position, are presented with suggestions for a wide variety of creative gymnastic activities including the development of routines. A stencil for drawing quick action figures is included in the set.

Norman, Randi, *Girls and Women's Gymnastics*. Dubuque, Iowa: Wm. C. Brown Company Publishers, 1965. Contains the excellent Scandanavian approach to gymnastics.

Prchal, Mildred, *Artistic Gymnastics—Floor Exercises*. Berwyn, Illinois: The author (2419 Scoville Ave., Berwyn), 1964. An excellent treatment of movement associated with floor exercises with some work on beam.

Sjursen, Helen, *Educational Gymnastics Series*. Waldwick, N.J.: Hoctor Records. This series completed in 1967 represents the first set of specialized books by a single author for women's gymnastics.

Szypula, George, *Tumbling and Balancing for All*. Dubuque, Iowa: Wm. C. Brown Company Publishers, 1957. The best book on tumbling in the English language. Some description of typical floor exercise movements.

Zabka, Norma (Editor), *Gymnastics Guide—1965-1967*. Washington D.C.: The National Education Assoc. (DGWS-AAHPER) 1201-16th St., N.W. Washington 36, D.C., 1965. Collection of articles on gymnastics by well-known authorities in the field of education, a majority of whom are women.

Many of the books listed will be found in the school library. If not, they can be ordered by writing to the companies and organizations listed in the references.

Enjoy the spice of movement. Participate vigorously. Learn to help others. Take a lesson from the champion. Your gymnastic initiation is thus complete. The best is yet to come.

Index

INDEX